# Health Communication and Sexual Health in India

```
T0132554
```

Over the past few years, ever since the advent of HIV & AIDS, there has been increasing discussion of the concept of sexual health. This upsurge is especially noticeable not only in the field of health education and promotion but also in academic sources. The recent discourse on sexual health is paralleled by an upsurge in the debate on sexual rights.

This book examines the social construction of sexual health in India through an analysis of HIV & AIDS messages. The broad objective of the book is to trace the growth and evolution of the concept of sexual health from a health communication perspective and to understand the role of the state in determining its form and structure. The methodology used includes comparative analysis of HIV & AIDS policies, document analysis on HIV & AIDS, poster and short films analysis, in-depth and open-ended interviews and case studies. The book shows that sexual health is constructed in various modes in India. The models that are elaborated are the medical model that constructs HIV scientifically and in terms of a compromised immune system; the epidemic model that identifies risk behaviours and transmission routes and the moralistic model. Social constructions of AIDS as plague or punishment against society are advanced by moralists who equate HIV with taboo social and sexual behaviour and the political constructions highlights public health in the face of obstacles to treatment and the delivery of services to people living with HIV.

Bringing together current research and discussions on the three areas of policy, practices and theoretical perspectives related to the use and social construction of sexual health through HIV & AIDS communication approaches with specific reference to India, this book will be of interest to academics in the field of health communication, HIV & AIDS, and South Asian studies.

**Ravindra Kumar Vemula** is Associate Professor and Head, Department of Journalism and Mass Communication, The English and Foreign Languages University, Shillong, India. His research interests are in development communication, health communication with special interest in HIV & AIDS, new media, communication policy and analysis. He has published extensively in indexed international journals and books. He is the co-chair of the HIV & AIDS and Communication Working Group of the International Association for Media and Communication Research (IAMCR). His latest book is *Health Communication in the Changing Media Landscape: Perspectives from Developing Countries* (2016) Palgrave Macmillan, *Global Transformations in Media and Communications Research* (A Palgrave/IAMCR series).

# Routledge Contemporary South Asia Series

For the full list of titles in the series please visit: https://www.routledge.com/
Routledge-Contemporary-South-Asia-Series/book-series/RCSA

**The Rule of Law in Developing Countries**
The Case of Bangladesh
*Chowdhury Ishrak Ahmed Siddiky*

**New Perspectives on India and Turkey**
Connections and Debates
*Edited by Smita Tewari Jassal and Halil Turan*

**The Judicialization of Politics in Pakistan**
A Comparative Study of Judicial Restraint and its Development in India, the
US and Pakistan
*Waris Husain*

**Employment, Poverty and Rights in India**
*Dayabati Roy*

**Bangladesh's Maritime Policy**
Entwining Challenges
*Abdul Kalam*

**Health Communication and Sexual Health in India**
Interpreting HIV and AIDS messages
*Ravindra Kumar Vemula*

**Contemporary Literature from Northeast India**
Deathworlds, Terror and Survival
*Amit R. Baishya*

**Land-Water Management and Sustainability in Bangladesh**
Indigenous practices in the Chittagong Hill Tracts
*Ranjan Datta*

**Dalits, Subalternity and Social Change in India**
*Edited by Ashok K. Pankaj and Ajit K. Pandey*

# Health Communication and Sexual Health in India

Interpreting HIV and AIDS messages

**Ravindra Kumar Vemula**

Routledge
Taylor & Francis Group

LONDON AND NEW YORK

First published 2019
by Routledge
2 Park Square, Milton Park, Abingdon, Oxon OX14 4RN

and by Routledge
52 Vanderbilt Avenue, New York, NY 10017

First issued in paperback 2020

*Routledge is an imprint of the Taylor & Francis Group, an informa business*

© 2019 Ravindra Kumar Vemula

*British Library Cataloguing in Publication Data*
A catalogue record for this book is available from the British Library

*Library of Congress Cataloging-in-Publication Data*
Names: Vemula, Ravindra Kumar, author.
Title: Health communication and sexual health in India : interpreting HIV and AIDS messages / Ravindra Kumar Vemula.
Other titles: Routledge contemporary South Asia series ; 126.
Description: Abingdon, Oxon ; New York, NY : Routledge, 2019. | Series: Routledge contemporary South Asia series ; 126 | Includes bibliographical references and index.
Identifiers: LCCN 2018019997| ISBN 9781138574656 (hardback) | ISBN 9781351273442 (ebook)
Subjects: | MESH: HIV Infections | Acquired Immunodeficiency Syndrome | Sexual Health | Health Communication | Health Policy | Social Determinants of Health | India
Classification: LCC RA643.86.I53 | NLM WC 503.7 | DDC 614.5/ 9939200954—dc23
LC record available at https://lccn.loc.gov/2018019997

ISBN 13: 978-0-367-58442-9 (pbk)
ISBN 13: 978-1-138-57465-6 (hbk)

Typeset in Times New Roman
by Taylor & Francis Books

**For my teachers**

# Contents

# Tables

# Acknowledgements

This research is an outcome of long and intense discussions in a classroom around two decades ago. Sex and sexuality are two contentious subjects in India, HIV & AIDS changed this perception and brought the entire debate into the public domain. This book is an attempt to seek answers to such questions, where the government itself gets into the mould of knowledge generator and disseminator for the masses on the aspects of sex, sexuality and ultimately sexual health.

I would credit this entire work to none other than to my teacher and supervisor, Prof. Vinod Pavarala. I am extremely grateful and indebted to him for making me what I am today—his perseverance has brought out the best in me. He has always been known as a person of rigour, professionalism and immaculate dedication as a teacher. We have always known him as a perfectionist. His professionalism as a mentor, his academic acumen and his sincerity of purpose helped me to work with honesty, integrity and commitment on this book. Prof. Pavarala has never compromised on the quality of work that he supervises. His enormous quota of patience, his unequivocal counselling and his unpretentious accessibility at every stage, made the work simpler and uncomplicated. I thank him profusely for giving me a sense of direction and allowing me to share my work at various conferences. On the whole, working with Prof. Pavarala on my doctoral research and this book has been a very rewarding and an insightful experience academically.

It was not as simple task as it looks on the surface to research and document about HIV & AIDS communication in India. The preliminary task was to trace people who had worked in the area of HIV & AIDS more than 30 years ago. This required an investigative acumen. All this became simple with the help of Dr. K. V. Srinivasan, Technical Specialist-STD, NACO, who guided me and acted as a link to other people who had worked with him on HIV & AIDS in late 1980s and early 90s. Though a few senior level people have moved onto other developing countries' HIV and AIDS programmes as country heads, their responses through email, questionnaires, etc. helped a lot. I would especially express my gratitude to Mr. Subba Reddy, Deputy Director-IEC, APSACS; Mr. Ananta Kumar Sahu, M & E expert, NACO and Shri. Sanjeev Kumar, communication consultant with NACO for the last

20 years for providing me an insightful enquiry into various aspects of HIV & AIDS campaigns, strategies and shifts. I will always be indebted to them.

This book would not have been possible without the help of so many people in so many ways. A special mention needs to be made about my friends and colleagues at the International Association for Media and Communication Research (IAMCR). I would like to express my gratitude to Prof. Purendra Prasad and Dr. Kanchan Kumar who believed in my abilities and motivated me regularly towards completion of this work. It is with immense gratitude that I acknowledge the support and help of Prof. Arbind Sinha of Mudra Institute of Communications, Ahmedabad (MICA) for giving me a sense of direction and purpose for my life. I would also like to thank all friends who supported me in completing this work successfully. I would also like place on record my appreciation to all the members of my school of Communication, English and Foreign Languages University, Hyderabad for supporting me wholeheartedly in my endeavour. Thank you—Mallika, John and Suchitra for standing by me at all times. A special mention for my friend and colleague—Hrishikesh Ingle, who painstaking worked, checked and rechecked the references.

On a personal front, this book would have remained a dream had it not been for Kranthi—my spouse, who stood by my decision of working on the book. Thanks—Kranthi, Karthikeya and Rithvik. I am also indebted to my parents—Shri. Gangadhara Rao and Smt. Uma Varalakshmi for their encouragement and support. I would also unequivocally express gratitude to my extended family members—Kiran Kumar and Shri. Ramana Rao.

# Abbreviations

| | |
|---|---|
| ABCD | Abstinence, Behaviour Change, Condom and Drugs |
| AIDS | Acquired Immune Deficiency Syndrome |
| ART | Anti-Retroviral Therapy |
| BCC | Behaviour Change Communication |
| CIDA | Canadian International Development Agency |
| CSW | Commercial Sex Workers |
| CVM | Condom Vending Machines |
| DFID | Department for International Development |
| FBOs | Faith-Based Organisations |
| FC | Female Condom |
| FSW | Female Sex Workers |
| GFATM | Greater Involvement of People with HIV & AIDS |
| GIPA | Canadian International Development Agency |
| GOI | Government of India |
| HIV | Human Immunodeficiency Virus |
| ICTC | Integrated Counselling and Testing Centre |
| IDU | Intravenous Drug Users |
| IEC | Information, Education, and Communication |
| ILO | International Labour Organisation |
| IMF | International Monetary Fund |
| IPPF | International Planned Parenthood Foundation |
| MHOFW | The Ministry of Health and Family Welfare |
| MSM | Men Having Sex with Men |
| MTCT | Mother-to-Child Transmission |
| NACO | National AIDS Control Organisation |
| NACP | National AIDS Control Programme |
| NCA | National Council on AIDS |
| NGO | Non-governmental Organisation |
| OVC | Orphans and Vulnerable Children |
| PLWHA | People Living with HIV & AIDS |
| PPLHIV | People Living with HIV |
| PPTCT | Prevention of Parent-To-Child Transmission |
| PSI | Population Services International |

| | |
|---|---|
| PWID | People Who Inject Drugs |
| RCH | Reproductive and Child Health |
| RTI | Reproductive Tract Infection |
| STD | Sexually Transmitted Disease |
| STI | Sexually Transmitted Infection |
| THRG | Targeted Interventions among High-Risk Groups |
| TI | Targeted Intervention |
| UNAIDS | United Nations Programme on HIV & AIDS |
| UNDP | United Nations Development Programme |
| VCTC | Voluntary Counselling and Testing Centre |
| WHO | World Health Organization |

# 1 Sexual health communication

## Policies and practices

Sexual health is a socially constructed phenomenon influenced by social norms, culture and personal experience. It is a complex and multidimensional construct (Lewis, 2004; Edwards & Coleman, 2004). All these factors affect the way individuals define, feel and perceive sexual health in their lives. There seems to be an upsurge in the use of the sexual health concept the world over in the recent past. Sexual health everywhere is understood in the framework of prevention—a public health-oriented domain of discourse concerned with prevention of disease. The preventive domain is the most dominant domain of discourse concerning sexual health. Prior to HIV & AIDS, research in preventive sexual health focused on areas such as unintended pregnancy and on sexually transmitted diseases (STDs) such as gonorrhea and syphilis. Sometimes it also addressed issues such as sexual debut. In the past two decades, HIV & AIDS has become the major focus of the preventive sexual health domain. This type of discourse is more concerned with identification of antecedents or risk factors to exposure to HIV and possible interventions to prevent exposure (Lewis, 2004). Historically, preventive sexual health was an extension of the public health approach to physical sexual health, which was more prominent in the sexual hygiene movements and its concern with the spread of venereal diseases (Hart & Wellings, 2002).

HIV & AIDS in its present manifestation centres on the identification of threats to public health, identification of risk and protective factors and the development, implementation and evaluation of interventions to promote public well-being (Lewis, 2004: 225). It is in this context that the World Health Organization/Pan American Health Organisation states that in order to construct an appropriate framework for the consideration of sexual health, basic concepts referring to sex and sexuality need to be defined and their definitions agreed upon (2001:5).

There seems to be little research regarding the ways in which sexual health is socially constructed and how it has got institutionalised after the advent of HIV & AIDS. This book is an attempt to explore the normative sexual health messages that have been socially constructed especially in India. It also attempts to investigate the social construction of sexual health in India, the various ways in which sexual health messages are created and disseminated through various media as part of the social discourse. In this book, attempts have been made to understand how the varied meanings of sexual health messages and safe sex practices have evolved, shaped and been socially constructed in the entire country. Such messages in turn influence the sexual behaviour of the population.

The social construction of sexual health pervades the academic arena as well as the popular media. In the past, research has focused on sexual health in terms of sexuality as family control, sterilisation and awareness about reproductive health, which are important topics, but all carry a socially constructed negative connotation. An understanding of the way people perceive, define and experience sexual health and how these variables affect individual's sexual health behaviour is needed. Much of the research in sexual health has been based on the sexual experiences of what society thinks is the norm: heterosexuality (Osmond & Thorne, 1993:616). Research studies are needed on how people understand and construct the sexual health messages in their lives. These kinds of studies should attempt deconstructing such constructs to critically understand the messages disseminated. Several papers on sexual health and its construction examine the depths and complexities of sexual health and its social construction thoroughly, but there is a need to study the concept in its entirety taking into consideration varied contexts which could be cultural, social or religious. This book also tries to explore the ways in which various cultural and societal norms, along with personal experiences and interpretations shape the sexual health messages, especially HIV & AIDS messages. From the constructionist position the process of understanding is not automatically driven by the forces of nature, but is the result of an active, cooperative enterprise of persons in relationship. In this light, inquiry is invited into the historical and cultural bases of various forms of construction on sexual health located in the existing body of knowledge.

It needs to be mentioned here that agencies that are involved in designing communication messages constitute subjectivities. This book focuses mainly on understanding how the discourse of the state dictates the normative sexual health practices. These diktats need to be understood keeping in mind the culture, the multi-textured messages, appropriating its available associations for its own message of the danger of AIDS. Since AIDS, unlike some other diseases that beset developing countries, cannot be controlled by public health strategies, such as by the improvement of sanitation or disinfecting facilities, one must explain it in other terms to have an impact on the psyche of the population. As a result of which they are forced to make an informed decision on what 'should' be right about their sexual health practice. Communication campaigns, through posters, TV, radio, teaser ads, exhibition panels, comic strips etc., attempt to bring in the psychological connection amongst the masses of what states thinks is normative sexual health. Discourses on normative sexual health, particularly emanating from authority structures, typically identify not only the source of 'disease'—AIDS —but how the messages are conceived. There is much debate on the cause of AIDS and the framework established for explaining the progression of the disease. Again, the device directs attention away from the socio-cultural features that spread and are rapidly spreading AIDS within the country.

## Defining sexual health

The World Health Organization (WHO) came up with the first internationally accepted definition of sexual health and published it in 1975. It was an outcome of a 1974 international technical consultation meeting held in Geneva. The technical report specifically targeted the health professionals and others involved in training programmes in the field of sexology. In a 1987 report, the WHO states that sexual health is not a scientific concept, but instead reflects an understanding of a culture that was tempered by the time and prevailing values (Edwards, & Coleman, 2004). In the same article they correlate the attempt to create a definition of sexual health with the attempts of establishing 'norms' for sexual health that are used to define people's behaviour as 'healthy' and others that do not fit the norms as 'unhealthy'. Such normative definition of sexual health does not take into account sexuality as a fluid phenomenon that changes with the ebb, flow of time, culture, relationship status as well as ethnic background. Thereby such kinds of definitions articulate an objective definition for sexual health that would inherently drive the future discussions (Edwards, & Coleman, 2004: 192). Thereafter, sexual health has been defined differently by different persons and organisations over the past many years and there is no universally agreed definition of sexual health (Coleman, 2002). Sexual health as a concept has relatively broadened from its narrow focus on biological functions to include social aspects (Barrett, 1991); similarly, there has been an expansion of the concept of sexual health from a focus on reproductive well-being and disease prevention to a broader integration of sexual well-being. However, a broader definition of sexual health has somehow has not led to changes in interventions, which continue to emphasise reproductive health and disease prevention markers as primary outcomes (Aggleton & Campbell, 2000). While sex is biologically determined, sexual behaviour is under social control. It is regulated by cultural constructs that identify the appropriate persons and circumstances with which and in which sexuality may be expressed. Regulation thus imbues sexual behaviour with social meaning by reinforcing and controlling the terms and conditions of interpersonal relationships and procreation (Sibthorpe, 1992). In the recent past, the understanding of the term 'sexual health' has evolved in a variety of ways. The definitions of sexual health the world over have been majorly influenced by the definition of health as envisaged by the WHO in 1946. Understanding of sexual health around the world is partly shaped by political, social and other historical events, such as the aftereffects of the 1960s sexual revolution, the ongoing struggle over reproductive rights and abortion, the maturation of gay rights movement, overpopulation concerns and the devastating international impact of HIV & AIDS (Edwards et al., 2004).

The definition of sexual health by the World Health Organization (2006:5) clearly states that:

> Sexual health is a state of physical, emotional, mental and social well-being related to sexuality; it is no merely the absence of disease, dysfunction or infirmity. Sexual health requires a positive and respectful approach to sexuality and sexual relationships, as well as possibility of having a pleasurable and safe sexual experience, free of coercion, discrimination and violence. For sexual health to be attained and maintained, the sexual rights of all persons must be respected, protected and fulfilled.

This definition of sexual health has some useful, broadly encompassing features. Sexual health is defined within a social framework, which need not have necessarily physical and mental aspects (Sandfort & Ehrhardt, 2004). Sexual health is defined in an affirmative way that stresses well-being and not the absence of negative qualities. This definition is more extensive than the WHO's definition in general, which was adopted in 1948. In its extension to sexual health, the definition is somewhat unclear: whose approach should be positive and respectful? Who is responsible for creating the possibility of 'having pleasurable and safe sexual experiences, free of coercion, discrimination and violence'[1] and fulfilling the sexual rights of persons? A further question is whose sexual health is being defined. It is in this background that this book tries to understand how sexual health is socially constructed through communication campaigns by the state agencies.

Sexuality is defined by the WHO (2006:5) as:

> Sexuality is a central aspect of being human throughout life and encompasses sex, gender identities and roles, sexual orientation, eroticism, pleasure, intimacy and reproduction. Sexuality is experienced and expressed in thoughts, fantasies, desires, beliefs, attitudes, values, behaviours, practices, roles and relationships. While sexuality can include all of these dimensions, not all of them are always experienced or expressed. Sexuality is influenced by the interaction of biological, psychological, economic, political, cultural, ethical, legal, historical and religious and spiritual factors.

It is obvious that the WHO's definition of sexual health is somewhat utopian. Who would qualify as 'sexually healthy' according to this definition? Given the worldwide prevalence of sexual prejudice, most if not all, sexual minorities would fail to meet the criteria. It seems that sexual health as defined by the WHO is more a worthwhile goal to aim for, rather than an adequate representation of most people's current condition. A more restricted definition might conceive sexual health as a prerequisite for people's (sexual) quality of life. In the WHO's definition, sexual health is defined in terms of a feature of an individual. The definition implies, however, an environment that can either be supportive of or impeding of someone's sexual health, suggesting that a macro level structural definition of sexual health would be feasible too. Sexual health would be a condition of an individual, relationship, or community, which facilitates various positive outcomes of sexual behaviour, without resulting in negative personal, relational, or societal consequences. The WHO definition, as well as other definitions of sexual health, implies psychological and societal norms about the expression of sexuality (Schmidt, 1987). Norms are clearly related to values and thus, such definitions of sexual health evoke the questions and concerns of whose values and beliefs are being determined and become regulated by the state. Another issue is the level at which these values are defined by the state. Traditionally, values were defined in terms of actual behaviour. Values can be defined more generally and abstractly in terms of how people interact with one another. The WHO definition avoids a specification of concrete behaviours, such as heterosexuality and homo-sexuality. The WHO adopts a more global ethical stance called a 'communicative sexual ethic' (Seidman, 2001). Seidman contrasts this with a normalising ethic that proclaims sexual acts having inherent moral meaning. This is an approach adopted by the government while formulating and implementing the campaigns on population control as well as HIV & AIDS in India. The basic focus of both programmes was on sexual health and its control. In a communicative sexual ethic, the focus of the normative evalua-tion shifts from the sex act to the social exchange. A global worldwide epi-demic, like HIV infection, that is largely caused by sexual behaviours might make it very useful to have a global definition of sexual health as a basis for prevention and care. Given its global stance, the WHO definition seems to be adequate for a worldwide adoption. Of course, this does not imply that the concept has the same relevance everywhere. Local adoption of the concept of sexual health requires knowledge of history and culture of a particular society and will always be strongly determined by specific social conditions, including religious and cultural values, as well as the category of people—in terms of age, gender, ethnicity, orientation etc. and its intersections—one is dealing with. The actual operationalisation of sexual health in policy documents varies and is affected by a variety of factors, including political and economic circumstances (Giami, 2002). In spite of all the caveats of cultural diversity that impact notions of sexual health, a clearly stated concept of sexual health may be useful, because such a concept offers a framework for thinking about goals to be accomplished and issues to be explored. It can help to organise research and action. It can also offer a framework for evaluating ongoing investigations and policies. Research typically deals with factors that promote, impede, or inhibit sexual health. A variety of factors can be explored, both for the individual and his or her direct environment (WHO, 2006). In terms of action, a definition of sexual health can help to conceptualise and specify goals for health policies, interventions, or advocacy.

## A brief theoretical overview

In the past, individuals had a responsibility for their own healthcare usually as a result of necessity. Families and communities shared their expertise and their beliefs. Only the relatively wealthy made use of professional services and the limited value of such services was well recognised. This gradually changed with the improved care and intervention provided by the health services and the free availability of such care to all. Although there was a widespread participation by the individual in local health care, there was little participation by the majority of the people in the development of policy towards health (McEwen, Martini & Wilkins, 1983). Few people, usually from a position of inherited status, wealth, or academic standing pursued active campaigns to improve health by a variety of measures amongst population. These were accompanied by a wide range of other humanitarian reforms led by the governments. When such measures were applied there was often little direct involvement by the public, but the public were the beneficiaries of such activities. Today, it appears that there is a different approach to improving the health and well-being of the population that reflects again the wider aspects of present social life. Traditionally, health education has been conceived as an asset within healthcare because it provides information and suggests alternatives to individuals, families, or groups to prevent disease and promote health. From this perspective, health education seems to be a 'healthy' practice, indeed 'good for you' (Gastaldo, 1997).

Health communication campaigns initially adhered to a narrow conceptualisation that focussed specifically on 'information transfer'. Mass media and interpersonal networks are seen largely as channels that 'transferred' such information. The dominant metaphor is one of communication as the transmission of information (Penman, 2000). The term 'target audience' categorically supported such linear, knowledge-to-attitude-to-behaviour effects models of communication. Messages were designed to be 'shot at' a target audience. The 'bullet theory or hypodermic needle theory' tersely had the underpinnings of an effects tradition in which the cathartic effect of the media on individuals was more. 'Classic' theories/models of health behaviour include: the health belief model, the theory of reasoned action, the trans-theoretical model, learning and conditioning, social learning theory, decision-making theory and diffusion of innovations (Collins & Rau, 2000). The primary objective of each is to predict and explain individual health-related behaviours. The trans-theoretical model posits 'stages of change' in which a person moves from 'pre-contemplation' to 'action' to 'maintenance' of behaviour change (Prochaska & Velicer, 1997). The trans-theoretical model advises that communication strategies should be tailored to an individual's level of inclination to change. The health belief model assesses a person's likelihood of undertaking a preventive health behaviour (such as getting an immunisation) based on the person's perceptions of susceptibility to disease, benefits of the proposed action and barriers to making the change. Most of the previously-mentioned models tend to emphasise the individual as a decision-maker, rather than the influence of the larger social context (Airhihenbuwa & Obregon, 2000). Of the dominant models, only the Theory of Reasoned Action and the Diffusion of Innovation approach include variables related to the influence of 'important others'. Health communication interventions ultimately tend to focus on expert-driven, risk-based information and rational decision making by individuals about discrete behavioural change (Guttman, 2000). Strategies that are used primarily for community interventions are interpersonal communication (individual advice or group counselling), mass media communication (print, television and radio) and a combination of both. Research into the use of mass media to improve public knowledge about health is one-dimensional because it focuses on what the most effective media channel—radio, newspapers, or television—do to create persuasive communications (Atkin, 1981). The degree to which healthcare values held by healthcare providers, the public and government coincided or conflicted was largely ignored in the campaign research literature of the 1970s and 1980s (Pettegrew & Logan, 1987). Conventional wisdom assumes that scientific knowledge is determined within the scientific paradigm, which is free and immune to the impact of social or cultural values. The transmission of information metaphor is so central in popular thinking, that it sometimes directs the government and its agencies to invest imprudently on highly unrealistic campaigns. Scientific theories and health knowledge are constantly influenced by the public, social and cultural values, which in turn may not have a reflection on the campaigns. Thereby the earlier communication planners need not be faulted for seeing media campaigns as a form to influence public education with only minimal loss of scientific data. Behavioural science since the early 1980s has made a major shift in health promotion toward a social-ecological paradigm, where attention is given to the impact of social norms, peers and family on individual behaviours. This kind of approach gets reflected in the new generation of multilevel health communication interventions. The narrowness of the models does not provide a sufficient understanding of why and how people (from diverse age, gender, cultural groups) make changes. It can be inferred that models may predict the 'attractiveness' of taking an action, but this is not sufficient to predict what people will ultimately do (Weinstein, 1993). The models do not provide 'testable predictions about the process that leads to behaviour change'. Further improvement of models will require a greater understanding of how mediating variables of behavioural change are affected by socio-cultural influences (Emmons, 2000).

### Objectives of health communication campaigns

Any campaign has broadly four objectives, which are inter-reliant and co-related a) exposure, b) infusion of information, c) change in behaviour, d) stimulation of interpersonal communication. The exposure achieved by disseminating campaign messages through multiple channels, for example, is expected to result in changes such as increased awareness about campaign-related issues, great levels of knowledge about health, higher levels of self-efficacy, and ultimately, healthier behaviours at both the individual as well as the broader community-wide levels. Campaign success depends on frequently reaching a broad cross-section of the audience with a clear message (Hornik, 1989). Although, the primary role of exposure in campaign success is indisputable, the mechanism through which exposure to campaign messages can lead to higher order changes has not received adequate attention. A clearer understanding of this mechanism is required to increase the likelihood that attaining the requisite exposure will lead to behavioural changes, which is the primary focus of most public health campaigns. Infusion of information into a society is seldom the only approach adopted by campaigns that seek to bring about long-term behavioural changes. Educational efforts also strive to stimulate individual's information-seeking skills so that the individual become an active and independent participant in seeking health information and using available channels in their community. Freire (1976) terms this process as 'empowerment'. The goal is to enable the receivers to take control of their own lives by providing relevant information. An operational understanding of empowerment by the state implies that by providing information to the society with a view to enabling it to understand the various policies of the state and derive benefits facilitating dissemination of information is central to the state's approach in different sectors including health. Empowerment can be defined as the process through which individuals acquire the knowledge and skills, that enable people to change themselves, their lifestyle, their environment, their perceptions about self and their relation to the social, cultural and political context. The resulting increase in awareness leads to a greater self-confidence and self-worth, thus decreasing self-alienation. These changes in self-regard increase the likelihood that the individual can in fact, through individual or group action, effect changes at all levels of this social world and become self-reliant. The enabling process begins with conscientisation and awareness of resources leading to increased knowledge through access to information. This is particularly germane for attaining improvement in long-term health that most public health campaigns, despite their temporary presence in the community, seek. Thus, one of the ways in which campaigners can enhance their effectiveness is by prompting individuals to seek additional information on their own. This can be achieved either by disseminating campaign messages that instruct and provide individuals with the requisite skills to seek health information or by increasing the health information available in the community. The ultimate goal of most health campaign is to change behaviour; evaluating campaign success according to this criterion appears reasonable. Kaplan (1990:1211) in fact argues, 'the only important indicators of Health and wellness are behavioural'. Secondly, a campaign-induced improvement in known behavioural precursors is also an indication of campaign success. For example, gain in knowledge about health as a result of exposure to a campaign. Possessing the requisite knowledge base, of course, does not always translate into behaviour. Without knowledge about risks and the means to reduce them, behaviour change is less likely to occur. Knowledge about the risks associated with a sedentary lifestyle, for example, will not necessarily translate into a physically active one, but without knowledge about the risks, it is unlikely that individuals will engage in a regular routine of physical activity. Hence, to the extent that a campaign results in knowledge gain, we can conclude that the campaign has facilitated behavioural change. Stimulation of interpersonal communication is another potential outcome of information campaigns.

Health and public health specialists primarily focus on the health needs of people and favour monitoring health to see how these needs are met. Their approach to impact analysis is therefore through monitoring health indicators and their changes. They would like to evaluate these changes in relation to predetermined health goals. Another factor that determines the extent to which individuals process health information is their level of involvement with the topic. As described by Salmon (1986) involvement is evident when an issue has significant consequences in people's lives. Freire (1976) proposes the process of 'conscientization' consisting of people's critical awareness of their own situation and development of each individual's aspiration for growth and self-realisation. Individuals highly involved with an issue not only engage in elaborate message processing (Petty & Cacioppo, 1986), but they also learn more from the message (Flora & Maibach, 1990) and make greater use of information compared to those whose level of involvement is low (Valente, Paredes & Poppe, 1998).

The basic objective of any Information, Education and Communication (IEC) campaign is to raise the awareness of community about health issues and to involve the people in the development process by assessing their needs. The increased awareness brought about by the campaign is expected to ultimately raise the demand for and utilisation of health services being provided by the health infrastructure. Although health communication reviews promote interpersonal discussion as a valuable campaign strategy (Flay & Burton, 1990), relatively few studies (Hafstad & Aarø, 1997; Meyer et al., 1980 as cited in Flay, 1987) have systematically investigated it as either an outcome of a campaign or a predictor of health behaviour change. Yet, interpersonal communication can effectively propagate campaign information (Valente & Saba, 1998), thus greatly increasing awareness about the reach of the campaign. Furthermore, although the mass media can serve to increase awareness about health issues, interpersonal discussions are instrumental in persuading people to make requisite behaviour modifications (Johnson & Meischke, 1993; Rogers, 2003). But, the major problem arises when the media components are not able to reach to the people they are meant for, because of their sporadic interventions. If indeed there is some potential for communication activities in development, why have current programmes using both conventional approaches and communication technology failed to realise their objectives? Does the fault lie with the receiver for adopting the innovation Hornik (1989)? And a majority of other scholars concur that the problem of sporadic information / awareness lies with the way information programmes or projects are conceptualised, designed and delivered. There is very little information flowing to the beneficiaries and much of it is not relevant to their needs and problems. Available studies suggest that conventional information distribution channels are typically weak. They may reach a small proportion of the potential audience for whom they carry information that is either outdated or unresponsive to the needs of the audience. Health and nutrition education is most often a burdensome addition activity for predominantly curative health services; ambitious outreach programmes atrophy with time (Hornik 1989). McGuire's (1989) communication / persuasion matrix was an attempt to delineate the various processes, starting from exposure required for a communication campaign to achieve behaviour change. The underlying assumption in McGuire's (1989) model—that a lower order process (e.g. knowledge gain) is required before a higher order one (e.g. behaviour change) can occur—is shared by many communication campaigns. This is one of the approaches adopted by prominent large-scale, community-oriented campaigns. In their theoretical review of media-based campaigns, Rogers & Storey (1987:836) observe, that 'widespread exposure to campaign messages is a necessary ingredient in communication campaigns effectiveness'. Acquiring the requisite amount of exposure is also the first major hurdle that public health campaigns have to overcome. Another proposition is whether, controlling for other known predictors, exposure to the awareness campaign material results in greater information seeking and interpersonal communication behaviours.

### Prominent health communication approaches

Health communication has changed dramatically over the last half century, passing through at least four different periods (Piotrow et al., 2003:1–2).

1    The clinic era, based on the 'Build it and they will come'—medical care model. The notion during this era was that if people knew where services were located they would find their way to the clinics.
2    The field era, where a greater emphasis was on outreach workers, community-based distribution and a variety of Information, Education and Communication (IEC) products like posters, leaflets, radio broadcasts and mobile units.
3    The social marketing era, premised on the fact that consumers will buy the products they want at subsidized prices. Highly promoted brands stimulated the demand side while convenient access through local shops and pharmacies expanded the supply side.
4    The era of strategic behaviour change communication founded on behavioural science models for individuals, communities and organizations. The primary emphasis of this approach was to influence social norms and

policy environments to facilitate and empower the iterative and dynamic process of both individual and social change.

As a result, the field of health communication has evolved and expanded greatly. From being initially a matter of high-volume production of simple print material—posters and brochures for clinics—communication has become a vital strategic component of health programmes. No longer simply repeating untested slogans like, 'A small family is a happy family' or providing pictorial instruction on why and how to use specific contraceptive methods, communication is now a vital and indispensable guide for many interventions. It represents not only the most conspicuous part of most preventive health programmes but also the strategic themes to enhance the importance of health programmes for policymakers and the public alike. Today, strategic communication can serve not only to increase the demand for specific preventive health services but also to motivate the suppliers of health services—providers at all levels—toward their commitment to serve their clients.

Many factors contributed to this growing emphasis on communication, including (Piotrow et al., 2003: 2–3):

- Growing evidence that well-designed communication interventions can have an impact on health behaviours and practices, not just knowledge and attitudes;
- A substantial expansion of mass media, new information technologies, and especially television to reach large audiences worldwide;
- The decentralization of health services, giving more power to local governments;
- Increased attention to the role of women, and other gender concerns;
- Emphasis on better quality, client-centred health care services, including counselling and client-provider communication;
- The spread of HIV & AIDS and growing recognition that child health and control of many emerging diseases may depend as much on individual and community behaviour as on medical technology; and
- The continuing search for behaviour change models that take account of complex interactions involving individual behaviour, community norms and social/structural change.

Communication continues to be one of the most important strategies in the fight against HIV & AIDS. In the absence of a vaccine or a cure, prevention is the most effective strategy for the control of HIV & AIDS. Around the world, the majority of the population is still uninfected. It, therefore, becomes imperative to continue intensive communication efforts that will not only raise awareness levels but also bring out behaviour change. There are basically two kinds of communication approaches that are being adopted by the National AIDS Control Organisation (NACO) to communicate sexual health to the masses; the Information, Education and Communication (IEC) approach which is basically a top-down approach and the other one, which boasts of being a bottom-up approach—the Behaviour Change Communication (BCC) approach. Information, Education and Communication is a process that informs, motivates and helps people to adopt and maintain healthy practices and life skills. It aims at empowering individuals and enabling them to make correct decisions about safe behaviour practices. Information, Education and Communication (IEC) also attempts to create an environment that is conducive and supports access to treatment and services for those already infected. In India, therefore, the development of appropriate and effective IEC strategies for HIV & AIDS is one of the biggest challenges not only in the health but also in the development sector. In the National AIDS Control Programme (NACP)-II, NACO has given the highest priority to an effective and sustained strategy to bring about changes in behaviour to prevent further infection. At the state level the IEC activities have been decentralised keeping in mind the need to respond to local priorities and communication in local languages. The objectives of the IEC strategy in the National AIDS Control Programme are (UNODC, 2006:86–87):

- To create a supportive environment for the care and rehabilitation of persons with HIV & AIDS.
- To raise awareness, improve knowledge and understanding among the general population about AIDS infection and STD, routes of transmission and method of prevention.
- To promote desirable practices such as avoiding multi partner sex, condom use, sterilisation of needles/syringes and voluntary donation of blood.
- To mobilise all sectors of society to integrate messages and programme on AIDS into their existing activities.
- To train health workers in AIDS communication and coping strategies for strengthening technical and managerial capabilities.

### Information, Education and Communication approach

Information, Education and Communication (IEC) combines strategies, approaches and methods that enable individuals, families, groups, organisations and communities to play active roles in achieving, protecting and sustaining their own health. Embodied in IEC is the process of learning that empowers people to make decisions, modify behaviours and change social conditions. Activities are developed based upon needs assessments, sound educational principles and periodic evaluation using a clear set of goals and objectives. The influence of underlying social, cultural, economic and environmental conditions on health need also must be taken into consideration in the IEC processes. Identifying and promoting specific behaviours that are desirable are usually the objectives of IEC efforts. Behaviours are usually affected by many factors including the most urgent needs of the target population and the risks people perceive in continuing their current behaviours or in changing to different behaviours. Health information is communicated through many channels to increase awareness and assess the knowledge of different populations about various issues, products and behaviours. Channels include interpersonal communication (such as individual discussions, counselling sessions or group discussions and community meetings and events) or mass media communication (such as radio, television and other forms of one-way communication, such as brochures, leaflets and posters, visual and audiovisual presentations and some forms of electronic communication). IEC has been associated with population and family planning programmes for a long time around the world. The United Nation Fund for Population Activities (UNFPA) was among the first to use the term in 1969 to label its communication activities. The terms 'birth control' and 'family planning' frequently were used in concern with the increasing populations. The traditional approach to IEC campaigns and community mobilisation used information to influence people's contraceptive behaviour according to policies generated by governments and population authorities (Colle, 2002). Population issues were linked to the AIDS situation, to providing assistance to infertile couples and to development in general. Along with these issues was the introduction of different approaches to reaching population including social mobilisation, social marketing, advocacy and interventions emphasising participation and empowerment. Within many agencies, the emphasis began shifting from agency-dictated goals to goals jointly determined by the agency (or government) and the broader health-related needs of the people. The Entertainment-Education (EE) approach has been used to promote family planning, gender equity and HIV & AIDS prevention in a large number of countries, including Nepal, India, Gambia, the Philippines, Tanzania, Mexico and Peru (Singhal & Rogers, 1999, 2001, 2002). Most of the campaigns were primarily carried out by two key organisations, Population Communications International (PCI) and The Johns Hopkins Center for Communication Programs and were funded by the United States Agency for International Development (USAID).

A white paper published by USAID locates its foreign assistance programme in the context of US security states the existence of many threats to national security in the post-Cold War, post-9/11 world. It felt that the US foreign assistance must address more than humanitarian and development goals. It should also address conditions of instability and insecurity that arise from terrorism, transnational crime, failing states and global disease that must be mitigated for sustained economic growth and social development to take root and flourish (USAID, 2004:7). Dutta (2006) suggests that one of the core goals of USAID is to support the project of transnational capitalism by opening up Third World spaces to foreign investment and the capitalist economy. Population growth in the Third World was seen as a barrier to fostering transnational capitalist ideology and thus the interventions sponsored by USAID focused on controlling population growth. It was argued that nations that controlled their population problem would be better able to manage their resources and citizens and would provide the recipe for a global climate for equitable growth. Population control serves transnational hegemony by fostering conditions for sustainable development, which in turn promotes economic growth and new opportunities for businesses. Population control programmes embody other ideological biases that underlie the conceptualisation. The attention has shifted onto serving the status quo by focusing on individual-level behaviour change among the subaltern classes, those undesirable groups whose vastly growing masses need to be managed and controlled (Dutta, 2006). The problem is located in the inability of the subaltern group to practice responsible and rational behaviours (e.g., planned reproduction). By focusing on population control as the solution to problems of global peace and stability, the funding agencies and interventionists privilege national and international elite positions, minimising and shifting attentions from the possibilities of real change in the condition of sub-alternity produced by practices of marginalisation and supporting the positions of elite privilege. The link between population control and marginalisation is evident in the programme of population control implemented in South Africa under apartheid that primarily targeted the Black population while encouraging increases in the White population by providing tax incentives for larger families and promoting immigration (Dutta-Bergman, 2004: 13).

During apartheid, contraceptive injections; sterilisations and fitting of intra-uterine devices was carried out on black women without their knowledge. Sometimes, they were not even allowed to sit for examinations if they had not submitted it (Correa, 1994). The political agenda of maintaining the wealth and access to resources in the hands of a small minority was further strengthened by the targeted approach in the population control programmes (Klugman, 1990).

### Behaviour Change Communication approach

Behaviour Change Communication (BCC) evolved as a multi-level tool for promoting and sustaining risk-reducing behaviour change in individuals and communities by distributing tailored health messages in a variety of communication channels. Behaviour Change Communication has many different, but related roles to play in the arena of health communication. Its primary focus is to increase knowledge. BCC has to ensure that people have the basic facts in a language, visual medium, or other media that they can understand and relate to. Effective BCC should motivate audiences to change their behaviours in positive ways. It should also stimulate community dialogue. Effective BCC should encourage community and national discussions on the underlying factors that contribute to the epidemic, such as risk behaviours, risk settings and the environments that create these conditions. BCC creates a demand for information and services, and spurs action for reducing risk, vulnerability and stigma. Apart from it, it also promotes advocacy. Through advocacy, BCC ensures that policymakers and opinion leaders approach the HIV & AIDS epidemic seriously. Advocacy takes place at all levels, from the national down to the local community level. BCC also has to play a main role in reducing stigma and discrimination. While communicating about HIV & AIDS, it addresses stigma and discrimination and attempts to influence social responses to them. Ultimately the main aim still is to promote services for prevention care and support. BCC can promote services that address Sexually Transmitted Infections (STI), Orphans and Vulnerable Children (OVC), Voluntary Counselling and Testing (VCT) for HIV, Mother-to-child transmission (MTCT), support groups for People Living with HIV and AIDS (PLWHA), clinical care for opportunistic infections and social and economic support. BCC can also improve the quality of these services by supporting providers' counselling skills and clinical abilities or can address to any of the epidemics. Table 1.1 differentiates both the approaches.

### Bio-power and health communication

Health education also represents a singular contribution to the exercise of bio-power (Foucault, 1978). Its involvement with prevention and health promotion, as well as its primary purpose of educating, enhance the set of power techniques that come into play in the management of individual and social bodies. Health education dates from the turn of the century, when the medical paradigm underwent a shift. In the nineteenth century, the predominant

*Table 1.1* Differences between IEC and BCC

| Themes | Information, Education and Communication (IEC) | Behaviour Change Communication (BCC) |
|---|---|---|
| **Information** | Message is sent or given, but the result is not expected | Change is expected |
| **Approach** | Top down | Bottom up |
| **Conveyed/ disseminated** | Through media (radio, newspapers) | Communicated directly to the targeted group |
| **Process** | One-way; no feedback from recipients | Two-way |
| **Relationship** | No relationships as messages are conveyed through indirect sources | Interpersonal relationship present |
| **Group** | Larger group | Smaller group |
| **Focus** | On a particular behaviour | Wide-ranging |
| **Better understood by** | Literate | Both illiterates and literates as it is through figures and photos |

model was 'hospital medicine', concentrating on symptoms and signs that together configured pathology. This model maintained its influence into the twentieth century, but gradually a new paradigm, 'surveillance medicine' has been recreating the concepts of health, illness and normality (Armstrong, 1995). Surveillance medicine moves the attention of medicine from pathological bodies to each and every member of the population. The categories of health and illness give way to the notion of risk—illness is not a problem per se, but a significant portion of health is redefined as an 'at-risk state' (Armstrong, 1995; Peterson, 1996). The borders between health and illness have also been reshaped—healthy people can become even healthier, and a person can be healthy and ill at the same time. The old tradition of teaching hygiene has proven to be insufficient and such aspect of change in behaviour has transformed into the promotion of health. (Armstrong 1995). Health education has become part of a whole strategy to promote health for all human beings, a strategy supported by the World Health Organization (WHO).

'In Foucault's view, biological life is a political event: population reproduction and disease control are central to economic processes and are therefore subject to political control' (Gastaldo, 1997:113). Foucault refers to biopower as a mechanism employed by the state to manage the population and discipline individuals. In this century, health has become increasing important politically as a major point of contact between the government and the population. Health education concentrates specifically on an individuals' responsibility for their own health and disease prevention, which was earlier called as 'traditional health education'. The practice that focused on empowering people to control their own health is called 'radical health education' (Gastaldo, 1997). The concept of radical health education figures in movements for health promotion, new public health and healthy public policy. It focuses on empowering people to control their own health. It is also committed to combating social inequality in a broad way and promoting community participation in health issues. Within this framework, health education can be seen as a political practice that enables individuals and groups in society to organise themselves to develop actions based on their own priorities (Gastaldo, 1997). Radical and traditional health educations share an underlying notion of empowerment through education or subjugation through ignorance. Both are based on the understanding that human beings are liberated beings unless something oppresses them; empowering them through education is a way to remove the 'chains' of oppression—ignorance, lack of political understanding, submissive behaviours, etc. What health education does construct is identity. Health education is an educational experience that gives professionals and patients/clients elements for building up representations of what is expected from 'healthy' and 'sick' people. These social roles are reinforced by a complex system of rewards and punishments. Health education is an intervention governed from the outside and a request of self-discipline of an individual. Intrinsically, it is a constructive exercise of power that improves the medical gaze; through the promotion of health, it circulates everywhere in

spheres that are new to bio-medicine. Health communication research programmes grounded in cultural theory have been advocated for a long time to
complement existing approaches (Tulloch, 1992).

> The development of praxis and the articulation of knowledge based on
> these dominant theories/models take for granted the voices of margin-
> alised people in the monolithically constructing them as the target audi-
> ence of persuasive campaigns based on 'universal truths' that are defined
> by dominant values, morals, and ideologies located in individual choice.
> Furthermore, these transmission-based theories/models that seek to
> modify individual behaviour via persuasion perpetuate violence on sub-
> altern spaces by imposing messages from outside that focus on changing
> cultural beliefs and practices.
>
> (Dutta-Bergman, 2004:238)

The culture-centred approach provides a point of departure from the dominant
approach by articulating the very absences in the dominant approach and by
emphasising context in the construction of health meanings. With their focus
on individual-level behaviour change, the dominant approaches fail to account
for the context that encompasses human existence and, therefore, silences the
voices of marginalised people by not including them in problem definition.
The health problem is preconceived by funding agencies and campaign scholars instead of being developed in dialogue with members of community. The
singular commitment to a particular behaviour constrains the ability of the
scholar to see the whole picture of health, to really understand the narrative and
to understand the 'real' risk faced by the people of the culture. Instead of
focusing on communicative meanings, the theories/models impose a dominant
worldview on the receiving population and erase the voices of cultural participants; the participation of the receiving population in formative and evolution
research serves the dominant framing of health problems rather than articulating
a community-based problem. Throughout history, nations and other organised
communities have attempted to use a variety of communicative tools, including oral and written persuasion, to guide, or as some would say control, social
change. Any constructive critique on health communication can also be located
amidst the very power structures within which development processes are
situated (Wilkins, 2000). Power structures may be conceptualised in a variety
of ways, such as through political-economic contexts and normative climate of
elite networks. This approach often takes the form of challenging development
discourse as a site of struggle over the representation of problems, communities
and solutions. Powerful development institutions conceptualise social problems in ways that benefits their own institutional and political-economic
interests. Daniel Lerner's (1958) quintessential treatise on the 'passing of traditional society' in the Middle East established a dominant framework for
understanding the relationship between media and modernisation. Lerner
proposed that media exposure would create more empathic individuals, who

would be able to imagine themselves beyond their local conditions, thus enabling them to participate in more democratic forms of political governance and more entrepreneurial economic activities. The literature of this historical period promoted a version of modernity that highlighted free-market capitalism, democratic governance, strong national identity (transcending cultural and ethnic differences) and faith in science and technology (e.g. Rogers, 1976; Schramm, 1963). In other words, the characteristics of the US at the time were proposed as a universal model for all other societies. By the 1970s, Asian and Latin American scholars began to critique the ethnocentric nature of this dominant approach. Critical scholars also recognised the limitations of seeing development as an isolated pursuit, drawing attention to the constraints in the global sphere that shaped development processes. As victims of cultural imperialism and dependency on wealthier nations, poor nations found it difficult to set autonomous development policies specifically on health, in accordance to their own cultural histories and societal interests. These and other critiques (e.g. Rogers, 1976) helped to open discussion in the field to considering alternative approaches to development. In response to a critique that the dominant model generally assumed a top-down flow of information, participatory approaches emphasised the importance of working at the level of local communities, with information generated at a local level disseminated to government agencies. Participatory approaches argue for local agency in defining both social problems to be addressed as well as determining appropriate solutions (Melkote & Steeves, 2001). Viswanath and Finnegan (2002) point out that low socio-economic status groups, which face the greatest threats of ill health, fail to benefit equally compared to higher socio-economic groups. The at-risk populations are most often left behind while campaigns continue to benefit the health rich. A substantive body of evidence on knowledge gap theory points out that health communication campaigns contribute to the existing gaps between the rich and the poor (Finnegan & Viswanath, 1997; Freimuth, 1990; Viswanath & Finnegan, 1995). Addressing the increasing societal chasm between the have and have-nots, health communication campaigns need to be reconfigured keeping in focus the need to serve the marginalised people (Marshall & McKeon, 1996). Such reconfiguration will demand a profound reflection on the capacity of campaigns to achieve behaviour change (Dutta-Bergman, 2004). This approach has been initiated within the fields of health communication and public health via novel individual campaigns efforts. Although the different alternatives to extant health communication approaches have been developed in the form of individual campaigns, they have hitherto been systematically integrated within a single framework and positioned against the backdrop of the dominant approach on the campaigns. Entertainment-Education campaigns are particularly suitable for this critique because they are implemented by Western interventionists in Third World spaces, reflecting the power differential in access to the discursive space between the West and the Third World and circulating the voices of the West in the formulation of the problems for the Third World.

## Health communication campaigns in India

The Universal Declaration of Human Rights, 1948, adopted and proclaimed by the UN General Assembly in Article 25 clearly states that that everyone has the right to a standard of living adequate for the health and well-being of himself and of his family, including food, clothing, housing and medical care and necessary social services, and the right to security in the event of unemployment, sickness, disability, widowhood, old age or other lack of livelihood in circumstances beyond his control. Whereas the assessment of National Health Reconstruction Mission (NRHM) carried out by the Ministry of Health and Family Welfare points to the fact that health is a state subject and the federal nature of the centre/state relationship ought to be factored in any central sector programme implementation (PIB, 2010). The primary responsibility for the design of the mission, and its implementation of any health programme in an effective manner, lies with the government. In an area as critical as healthcare, time is of the essence. Constant and persuasive direction and guidance from the ministry would be required so that implementation of programme activities by the states is both effective and expeditious. Given that the ministry is directly intervening at the district level through various societies and infusing large sums of money to build both physical and human resources capacities, it is important for the ministry to provide effective overall leadership for the mission so that the its goals are achieved and the implementation of the activities are not beset with the difficulties that have affected the implementation of central sector programme in the past.

After independence, India embarked on ambitious Five-Year Plans for development, which aimed at both long-term and short-term planning. The First Five-Year Plan (1952–57) brought the realisation to the policymakers that the uncontrolled population growth was the real culprit behind the failure of the plans. Population control was the first prominent issue to be addressed by the media experts, superseding other life-threatening diseases. As a result of which, India became the first country in the world to announce an official Family Planning Programme. When Indian Prime Minister Nehru presented India's first population-limitation policy in December 1952, the population establishment found a willing government that would allow them to start experimenting on its people to find a cheap contraceptive 'to be used in poverty-stricken slums, and among the most ignorant people' (Connelly, 2009). As the initiatives gained unstoppable momentum, the brutal consequences shocked even the most enthusiastic population controllers.

During the Fifth Five-Year Plan, the Government of India executed an agreement with the Advertising Agency Association of India to design a communication strategy for the states of Uttar Pradesh, Andhra Pradesh and West Bengal and this agreement is still considered a landmark in evolving communication strategies in the Family Planning Programme. The objectives of the strategy were to provide appropriate knowledge about methods of contraception, allay fears among the people, provide accurate information as to where one can have family planning services, and finally stimulate inter-personal contact. The entire thrust of health communication strategies in India emanates from the deliberation based on three premises: i) stratification of the population on the basis of qualitative and geographical characteristics and then attempting to elicit behavioural change by devising special schemes of IEC; ii) information dissemination will be necessity driven; iii) use of media to be decided after studying the media consumption patterns of the people to be communicated with health related information. It was further decided that the planning of all schemes would be done at the district level and implementation at the village or local level. Central government would only help in the facilitation of the scheme. This obviously needed a more region-specific IEC policy (Goswami, 2007). India carried out campaigns in various health, nutrition and population programme areas such as family planning, leprosy, tuberculosis, malaria, leprosy, mother and child health and polio etc. to name a few, after its independence in 1947 and during the implementation of the Five-Year Plans.

Population control campaigns have always been dubbed as a major failure, because population in India does not seem to abating ever since population control campaigns started. The scheme started with the concept of a small family and the raging slogan: *Hum do hamare do* (We two and ours two). A red inverted triangle symbol was conceptualised during the Fourth Five-Year Plan (1969–74) as a branding effort to familiarise and popularise the idea of family planning in India. Similarly, social messages such as 'Small family is a happy family' kinds of messages were disseminated amongst the masses that led to wider acceptance for limited family size. These messages were success-ful in sensitising the people, but their impact is difficult to assess primarily because the benefits inbuilt in these messages were intangible and could only be realised at a later stage, unlike commercial messages that promote commodities (Goswami, 2007).

The use of communication by the leprosy programme in India offers valu-able lessons for other programmes, both in terms of its successes as well as the challenges it threw up. It has raised awareness about the signs and symptoms of leprosy and the importance of seeking early treatment, and reduced the social stigma associated with the disease. 'Early efforts at communication in leprosy were hampered by the lengthy treatment of uncertain outcomes and limited media options' (Mukherji et al., 2006:ix). The Modified Leprosy Elimination Campaigns (MLECs) scaled up interpersonal communication and made use of mass media in the programme. Communications efforts helped enormously to promote belief in the curability of leprosy, increase community awareness of the free availability of treatment and diminish the stigma associated with the disease. The introduction of the drug Rifampicin as a part of multi-drug therapy (MDT) could finally offer shortened treatment durations and a cure and helped enhance the credibility of the programme among patients and the community. On the other hand, tuberculosis (TB) was another major public health problem in India. India accounts for one-fifth of the global TB incident cases. Since 1993, the Government of India (GoI) has been implementing the WHO-recommended Directly Observed Treatment Course (DOTS) strategy via the Revised National Tuberculosis Control Programme (RNTCP). Communication campaigns have worked in tandem with the government in informing people about it and bringing down the prevalence levels of TB all around the country. The increasing rate of HIV infection in many countries has had an impact on tuberculosis (TB) epidemiology as well. While TB prevalence has remained stable, TB incidence continues to rise, especially in countries most severely affected by the HIV epidemic as well as those facing political turmoil, migration, poverty and unemployment and where intravenous drug abuse is rampant (Swaminathan & Narendran, 2008).

Similarly, the National Malaria Control Programme was implemented in the India from 1953 to 1958, which later got converted into eradication programme. Aggressive campaigns using DDT were launched in India, leading to the rapid eradication of malaria. This DDT campaign was backed up media messages through radio, wall frescos and through village-level health workers. Though the campaign was unsuccessful in eradicating malaria completely from India, it did achieve tremendous reductions in malaria prevalence (Cutler et al., 2007). Pulse Polio is an immunisation campaign established by the Government of India in 1995–96 to eradicate poliomyelitis (polio) in India by vaccinating all children under the age of five years against polio virus. In 1995, following the Polio Eradication Initiative of the World Health Organization (1988), India launched Pulse Polio Immunisation Programme along with the Universal Immunisation Programme, which aimed at 100% coverage. Till date, the Pulse Polio campaign is counted amongst the most successful health communication campaigns in India. The entire programme made use of all the available media resources and was successful in reaching out to parents with young children below five at a place near them.

With the advent of HIV & AIDS, health concerns got an international angle. HIV seems to be falling in that parameter, where it affects everyone in world unmindful of where they come from. HIV & AIDS also initially carried the 'foreign' tag along with it, therefore the international concerns were very high because of its primary transmission mode (i.e. sexual intercourse). The same cannot be attributed to other diseases discussed previously such as malaria, leprosy, TB or polio, which continue to pose long-standing health challenges for India. Thus, international concern is not pertinent. Therefore, many of the developed countries made it mandatory for tourists arriving in their countries to have had the requisite vaccinations for those diseases. HIV & AIDS reversed this trend. HIV & AIDS also saw unprecedented inflow of foreign funds that no other life-threatening disease witnessed which was at the same time corroborated by the mainstream media images imported from the Western world. Thus, HIV & AIDS progressed to be the first ever 'televised disease'. HIV & AIDS is the first epidemic of the information age and as such has been widely reported on by the media due to its newsworthiness. This allows the media to be significantly involved in defining images of HIV & AIDS using sophisticated information technologies to target people (Connelly & Macleod, 2003). HIV & AIDS was originally steered by WHO, it became the only disease with a dedicated UN agency: the joint programme of HIV & AIDS (UNAIDS).

## Note

1  www.who.int/topics/sexual_health/en/ accessed on 4/8/18.

# 2 Politics of sexual health communication in India

## Perspectives

### History of sexuality in India

The seeming contradictions of Indian attitudes towards sexual health can be best explained through the context of history. India played a significant role in the history of sex, from writing the famous literature on sex and sexuality (*Kamasutra*) that treated sexual intercourse as a science. This literature went onto be the philosophical focus of new-age groups' attitudes on sex. The *Rig Veda,* one of the most revered *Vedas,* reveals a moralistic perspective on sexuality, marriage and fertility. In his article, 'Concerning Kamasutras: Challenging narratives of history and sexuality', Puri (2002: 632) observes that *Kamasutra* was primarily a mode of regulation and control of sexuality, not through a consideration of pleasure but as a way of channelling sexual behaviour in a hierarchical social setting. After the births of the Buddha and Mahavira, and the writing of the *Upanishads* around 500 BC, further historical evidence, art and literature shows that ancient Indian society was perhaps as sexually tolerant as many modern European and East Asian countries. At the end of the medieval period in India and Europe, colonial powers such as the Portuguese, British and French found ways of reaching India, where they allied with various post-Mughal Indian kings, and later managed to annex India. The arrival of the British had the largest effect on the culture of India and its attitudes towards sex and sexuality. Early British exposure to India occurred at a time when Europe was entering the Age of Reason, and so, whilst there was a lot of Protestant discrimination of Hindu beliefs and Indian society along the lines of early Muslim invaders, there were also a significant number of Orientalists who saw India as a great civilisation and invented the field of Indology. However, the main moral influence that led to stigmatisation of Indian sexual liberalism by Indians themselves was the Victorian value system. The effects of British education, administration, scholarship of Indian history and biased literature all led to the effective 'colonisation' of the Indian mind with European values. Nirad Chaudhuri in his landmark book *Continent of Circe* focuses on the concepts of morality of Europeans. He states that the Europeans were shocked particularly when Hindus mixed up sexual experiences with the spiritual. This seemed wholly unnatural to them, which they could not reconcile with the principle of morality familiar to them (Chaudhuri, 1966: 104). This led some Indians to seek conformity of their religious practices and moral values with those of Victorian era. Countries such as India became more conservative after being influenced by European ideas. At the same time, translations of the *Kamasutra* and other 'exotic' texts became available in Europe, where they gained notorious status, and ironically may have triggered early foundations of the sexual revolution in the West.

India's initiation to sexual health messages may have started with the colonial concerns with syphilis and gonorrhea amongst its armed forces. Britishers were also concerned with the behaviour of the prostitute women who were solicited by its forces (Levine, 1994: 581). The colonial enactments aimed at controlling female prostitution and curbing venereal disease, especially among the British military, differed in important respect from their domestic cousins. Two major legislative measures were enacted by the British after the 1857 mutiny[1] viz., 1) The Umbrella Cantonments Act (Act XXII of 1864), which organised and regulated the sex trade within the military cantonments that attempted to regulate commercial sex activity in the military towns; and 2) The Indian Contagious Diseases Act (Act XIV of 1868), which enacted similar provisions for the supervision, registration and inspection of prostitute women in major Indian cities and seaports. The colonial regime during their self-rule period post 1857 promulgated awareness-generation material on syphilis and gonorrhea to be circulated among its armed forces. Levine also highlights how the heightened awareness of the existences of female prostitution amongst the British authorities at home and in India, brought about a complex mix of moralism, sanitary regulation and military lobbying. The mid-century abounded with pamphlets, sermons, books and periodical articles about the social evil (Levine, 1994: 581). According to *Medical History of British India*,[2] Lock hospitals came into existence after the 1857 mutiny that specialised in treatment of venereal diseases especially syphilis amongst the British armed forces. The term 'Lock Hospital' dates back to the days of leprosy, based on the 'locks' or the rags which covered the lepers' lesions. Lock hospitals were provided in India following the introduction of the Contagious Diseases Acts of 1864 and 1868. Venereal disease was more prevalent amongst the British army than the civilian population, but there is no recorded data about any decline in the spread of venereal disease among the British soldiers. Fines were imposed on native women if they practiced prostitution without registration or if they failed to attend the examination.

Post-independence in 1947, India embarked on the ambitious population control programme, which focused solely on the individual's sexual practices and behaviours (detailed in the next section). Throughout the decades following the implementation of India's Family Planning Programme in the 1950s, the prevailing idea in dealing with overpopulation has been that drastic measures needed to be undertaken. Education regarding temporary methods of contraception was neglected in favour of encouraging sterilisation. Government agencies would have sterilisation quotas to fill among the employees, and the inability to meet them was sometimes met with withholding of the salaries (Bose, 1998). Workers were often rewarded with a radio or television if they successfully convinced enough people to opt for the surgery. At its worst, India's policy included declaring a state of emergency in 1975 and implementing forced sterilisation in poor neighbourhoods. When applying for government loans or jobs people were told that their chances of receiving such aid would be increased if they could produce a certificate of sterilisation. The national focus on sterilisation seems to have created an 'all or nothing' mentality among Indians towards birth control especially since the awareness of other, temporary methods of contraception for much of the twentieth century was miniscule. In a 1993 study, India's National Family Health Survey, revealed that of all contraceptive use at the time, 67% was by female sterilisation (compared to 9% male sterilisation)[3]. The prominence of female sterilisation indicates another flaw in India's population control strategies. By targeting women instead of men, the government inadvertently opted for the more hazardous means of birth control. The surgical procedure is more difficult and the rate of failure is high, not to mention the danger to the patient, which sometimes meant death. Upon learning of these semi-forced, safety-negligent policies, a fairly accurate explanation can be given on why family planning efforts have failed to curb rampant population growth in India. Asish Bose, in his book, *From Population to People,* states that the family planning programme could not succeed because India started it at the wrong end. He points to the fact that the primary clients were women towards the fag end of their reproductive lives. This happened because the population control programs relied heavily on the terminal methods of sterilisation, which could be an easy solution but may not be the best one. The miniscule successes in the sterilisation programme were either due to coercion or due to extreme poverty of the acceptors who look upon the family planning incentive money as paltry contribution to their poverty reduction (Bose, 1998: 115). When the only option available to many people is one that is irreversible, not to mention potentially life-threatening, people would probably be inclined to opt for no contraceptives at all. In such a scenario, the problem was not solved and the population kept growing and resources per head kept dwindling.

## The National Population Control Programme in India: Initiation of sexual health control

Though some sort of population policy was implicit in the First Five-Year Plan, it was only from 1966 onwards when a new Department of Family Planning was carved out in the Ministry of Health that serious thought was given to the implementation of a population control programme. The philosophy behind the programme was based on a Western model (under the influence of foreign donor agencies) involving payment of money (on the pretext of paying compensation) to the acceptor. Faint beginnings of the birth control movement in India can be traced to the early twenties of the nineteenth century. Beginning with the attendance of Indian representatives at the first international birth control conference in London in 1922 and the New York birth control conference in 1925, the birth control movement in India became progressively more organised until its culmination in the formation of the Family Planning Association in India in 1949. The National Family Planning Programme was launched in 1951 with the demographic objective of reducing birth rates to the extent necessary to stabilise population at a level consistent with the requirements of the national economy. During the first decade of its existence, family planning was considered more a mechanism to improve the health of mothers and children than a method of population control (Visaria, 2000; Visaria & Chari, 1998). Clinic-centred family planning service delivery, along with health education activities, was promoted during this period. The Third Five-Year Plan period (1961–66) marked a subtle shift in programme emphasis, from the welfare of women and children to the macro objective of population stabilisation (Visaria and Chari, 1998). An extension-education approach replaced the original clinic-centred approach and the programme was integrated with existing health services during this period. During 1965–75, the programme was integrated with the maternal and child health programme, and at the same time, time-bound method-specific targets for population control were introduced. As is well-known, the target-oriented approach became highly coercive during the State of Emergency in India (1975–77). The backlash of the coercive approach compelled subsequent governments to stress the voluntary nature of the family welfare programme. In the 1980s, the time-bound, target-oriented approach was revived with greater emphasis on promoting reversible methods and measures for child survival. As a part of the strategy, incentive payments for acceptors and motivators of contraceptive methods were vigorously promoted (Visaria, 2000). The 1990s witnessed dramatic changes in the family welfare policy and programme in the country. The passing of the 72nd and 73rd Constitutional Amendments and Panchayati Raj and Nagar Palika Acts in 1992, set in motion the process of democratic decentralisation, and brought in the family planning programme, legally, in the domain of Panchayati Raj institutions. In addition, several factors including the stagnation in the family planning programme, organised pressure from multiple constituencies to address issues of quality and choice, and the recognition of inherent constraints in the programme contributed to changes in policy approach (Visaria, Jejeebhoy, & Merrick, 1999). An additional catalyst was provided by the International Conference on Population and Development (ICPD) in 1994 and the Beijing Women's Conference in 1995. In 1996, the government took the radical decision of eliminating method-specific contraceptive targets that had been used to guide, monitor and evaluate the programme for decades, replacing it with what was initially called the target-free approach, where goals are set at the community level rather than determined at the centre. In 1997, the target-free approach was recast as the Community Needs Assessment Approach, and a decentralised participatory planning system was put in place. It was during the Fourth Five-Year Plan when communication efforts became truly effective in India. The now famous 'Red Triangle' symbol for family planning was conceived during this period and a national campaign was launched for advocating 'two or three children—enough'. The campaign for male contraception—the condom under the brand name *Nirodh* was the first social marketing effort undertaken with professional guidance was also initiated about this time. There was a setback after 1975–76 due to the negative impact of mass sterilisation camps. The programme was renamed as the National Family Welfare Programme, which began to address not just contraceptive needs, but also child-survival and maternal-health issues. Thereafter, the programme encompassed many areas of reproductive and child health and a multimedia approach was used to disseminate information. In the wake of the country's acceptance of the global agenda of ICPD (Plan of Action)—1994, the Government of India launched the Reproductive and Child Health (RCH) programme in 1997. This represented a radical shift in the government's policy as it moved away from obsession with sterilisation targets, to a bottom-up decentralised participatory planning process based on community needs assessment. The programme covered an extended range of services for unwanted fertility, maternal health, Reproductive Tract Infection (RTI)/ Sexually Transmitted Infection (STI), child health and adolescent health. The new paradigm embodied in the RCH programme generated a strong demand for new initiatives in the Information, Education and Communication (IEC) campaign. The Ministry of Health and Family Welfare (MHOFW) engaged private professional agencies to produce audiovisual software for the programme. It also invited eminent filmmakers to make full-length feature films on RCH issues. The RCH paradigm shift was towards client-centred, demand-driven services that needed strategic communication. It was as a tool to create demand for quality services. The communication challenge for RCH was one of demand creation and this required understanding of media opportunities, professional procedures and the use of social marketing approaches. The focus was no more on awareness generation; the communication campaign had to promote behavioural change. In January 1999, MOHFW started the process of defining a holistic and yet flexible strategy for communication of the country's RCH programme. Starting with a National Workshop in January 1999, followed by three Regional Workshops in the summer of 1999 and a series of deliberations, the National Communication Strategy was adopted through a National Workshop in October 2000. The strategy laid down the goals and suggested an operational framework for communication at the central, state and district levels. It also identified the major behavioural change objectives that the communication managers had to address and achieve along with the barriers and opportunities that were in place. A crucial feature of the new strategy is the recognition that, increasingly, IEC work will have to be taken over by the states, districts and community leaders. The central government continued to play the lead role in the national mass media campaign and multimedia campaigns, while the local radio, TV and print media and local specific IEC work through leaflets, posters, traditional entertainment methods, banners, hoardings etc. were the exclusive responsibility of the state, district and community. The massive IEC campaign for social mobilisation for Pulse Polio Immunisation over the last few years is one such significant activity undertaken by the state. One of the most important lessons learnt from the polio campaign has been the realisation that at the field level, Inter-Personal Communication (IPC) is the key to behavioural change. The mass media creates an enabling environment that lends credibility to what the health worker is saying. The crucial factor is to make the people come to the booth for the vaccine, which in turn depends on the persuasive skill of the health worker. The National Population Policy (2000) stresses that the family welfare messages have to be clear, disseminated everywhere and be in local dialects. It emphasises the need for inter-sectoral convergence for IEC and sensitisation of all field-level functionaries. It also encourages advocacy and sensitisation of the opinion leaders. It clearly states that all methods and means of communications are important. What needed to be decided was the right mix and the appropriate levels on which the campaign could be carried out. Growing partnership with NGOs and with the private sector for social mobilisation and IEC had become essential for success.

## National STD and AIDS Control Programme and policy in India

The National Sexually Transmitted Disease (STD) Control Programme was initiated in 1946 (before India's independence) and remained operational until 1991. However, the programme was weak both in terms of content and implementation. Following reports of the first HIV case in the mid-1980s and the emergence of HIV & AIDS epidemic, the National AIDS Control Programme was launched in 1987. In the initial years, the programme focused on raising public awareness, screening of blood for transfusion, and conducting surveillance activities in the epi-centres of the epidemic (NACO, 2002a). Recognising the synergy between STIs and HIV & AIDS, in 1992, the National STD Control Programme was integrated with the National AIDS Control Programme (NACO, 1999). The National AIDS Control Project (NACP) was launched in the same year. The thrust of the project was on changing behaviour through interventions, particularly among high-risk groups, supporting decentralised service delivery and protecting human rights by encouraging voluntary counselling and testing and discouraging mandatory testing (NACO, 2003). The National AIDS Prevention and Control Policy (2002) envisaged effective containment of the infection levels of HIV & AIDS in the general population in order to achieve zero level of new infections by 2007. In order to meet these objectives, the policy delineated various strategies including raising awareness, controlling STIs, ensuring the safety of blood and blood products, improving services for the care and support of people living with HIV & AIDS, and creating an enabling socio-economic environment. The policy reflected the paradigm shift, and emphasised on the importance of inter-sectoral coordination, forging partnerships with multiple stakeholders including NGOs and community-based organisations, decentralised planning and implementation, and integration of services. It recognised that the HIV & AIDS must be seen not only as a public health issue but also as a problem of development. Every country in the world has been affected by HIV & AIDS. In response, most countries have established a national AIDS programme and have conducted massive awareness campaigns through the mass media and other available platforms. (WHO, 1994). The precise impact of the mass media on reducing AIDS risk behaviour is continually debated, knowledge about AIDS is obtained most often from mass media rather than from interpersonal sources (Ross & Carson, 1988). Since its beginning, the HIV & AIDS epidemic has led to the infection of millions worldwide, prompting countries to craft policies and institutions aimed at containing the spread of the disease. The epidemic had manifested itself both as a precise problem but also as an all-encompassing one. Its precision is revealed in its associated morbidity and mortality in increasing number of people—mostly otherwise healthy, productive, young people—getting sick and dying (Cohen, 2002; Collins and Rau, 2000). The response to the first two decades of the epidemic addressed this quality of the crisis. It focused on the epidemic as a health crisis and on its ramifications for health service delivery. The aftermath of deaths due to HIV began to permeate and affect every facet of life and national development in the regions most affected (Stillwaggon, 2000; Poku, 2001). Death due to AIDS brought with it loss of productive resources as well as a sharp decline in economic production (Donahue, 1998; Mutangadura, 2000). The most common means of HIV transmission is through unprotected sex. Other transmission routes include mother-to-child transmission at birth, sharing contaminated syringes and needles through injection drug use and, to a lesser extent, the transfusion of infected blood and blood products. In June 2001, the United Nations General Assembly Special Session (UNGASS) on HIV & AIDS set in place a framework for national and international accountability in related to the epidemic. Each government pledged to pursue a series of benchmark targets relating to prevention, care, support and treatment, impact alleviation and children orphaned and made vulnerable.

### The evolution of the HIV & AIDS programme in India

Since the first case of HIV & AIDS was reported in 1986, the Government of India has addressed the epidemic with concern and resources. The Ministry of Health and Family Welfare constituted the National AIDS Committee in 1986, under the chairmanship of the Union Ministry of Health and Family Welfare.

The Committee brought together various ministries, Non-Governmental organisations (NGOs) and private institutions for effective coordination of programme implementation. With the support from the WHO, a medium-term plan was developed. The initial activities focused on the reinforcement of programme management capacities as well as targeted education and awareness campaigns (IEC) and surveillance. A comprehensive five-year (1992–97) strategic plan, the Prevention and Control of HIV & AIDS Phase I, was prepared by the Government of India. This brought about the establishment of the National AIDS Control Organisation (NACO). During this stage, activities focused on preventing transmission of HIV through blood and blood products, control of hospital infections, increasing awareness of the dangers of unsafe sexual behaviours with multiple partners and sharing of needles for injecting drugs and strengthening of clinical services for both STIs and HIV & AIDS (World Bank, 2003; NACO, 2005). State AIDS societies were formed to reduce the bottlenecks of implementation of the programme, with decentralised administrative and financial power for more focused implementation to address the issues at the local level. Phase II of the National AIDS Control Programme (NACP) began in 1999. NACO assumed the responsibility for activities such as epidemiological surveillance for STIs and HIV & AIDS, training and capacity building, operational research and monitoring and evaluation. NACO is also responsible for policy-level guidance, overseeing of the programme, allocation of public funds to the states, approval of proposed control activities and coordination with other donor partners. NACO works closely with states and coordinates advocacy meetings. In 2002, the government finalised and released the National AIDS Control Policy and the National Blood Policy Document. These policies were drafted following a wide range of consultations with government organisations (GOs) and NGOs, experts and partner agencies (Over, 2004). The main strategy in India to implement targeted intervention is to work through NGOs. The State AIDS Control Societies had identified 930 NGOs to deliver targeted interventions among high-risk groups. The interventions are aimed at commercial sex workers (CSW), migrant workers, truckers, street children, men having sex with men (MSM), intravenous drug users (IDU) and prisoners, mainly to decrease transmission by reducing high-risk behaviours. The AIDS control programme till date has been carried out in three distinct phases, which have been elaborated later in this document. The fourth phase (2012–17) was completed recently.

### National AIDS Control Programme I

The National AIDS Control Programme **Phase-I (1992–99)** was implemented across the country with an objective to slow the spread of HIV to reduce future morbidity, mortality and the impact of AIDS by initiating a major effort in the prevention of HIV transmission. It started with an International Development Association Credit of $84 million USD from the World Bank

(NACO, 2006; Chhabra, 2007). The basic aim of this phase was awareness generation regarding HIV & AIDS. The NACP-I focused on initiating a national commitment, increasing awareness and addressing blood safety. It achieved some of its objectives, notably an increased awareness. Professional blood donations were banned by law. Screening of donated blood became almost universal by the end of this phase. The programme had also established a decentralised mechanism to facilitate effective state-level responses by 1999, although substantial variation continued to exist in the level of commitment and capacity among states. Whereas states such as Tamil Nadu, Andhra Pradesh (undivided) and Manipur demonstrated a strong response and high level of political commitment, many other states, such as Bihar and Uttar Pradesh, were yet to reach these levels. This programme led to the capacity development at the state level with the creation of State AIDS Cells in the Directorate of Health Services in states and union territories (World Bank, 2003).

A mass IEC programme was launched to create public awareness of HIV & AIDS. This was done by using various media and aiming at different audiences from the general public to school children. Public information campaigns were launched that actually spoke of how HIV infection was acquired and how it wasn't, through casual contact, for example. Some of the campaigns were based on the ill-advised principle of preventing people from behaviour that put them at risk of HIV infection, by making them afraid of it. It was common to find early awareness messages with fear-provoking images such as skull and crossed bones. Such campaigns were to lead to the long-term problems of AIDS phobia and stigma and discrimination of infected people at all levels including at healthcare facilities. Rs. 75 Crores was spent on communication campaigns in one year (VHAI, 2001, as cited in Chhabra, 2007:6). The government during this phase felt that condoms were the only method with which HIV could be controlled. Thus, the condom was repositioned again in the context of HIV & AIDS. The condom, as discussed earlier, was used effectively as a tool for 'population control', now the same commodity had been reintroduced as a tool for sexual awareness and concerns. A detailed analysis of the entire gamut of condom discourse has been elaborated in Chapter 6. As a whole, condoms were known to be effective in preventing the transmission of HIV and other STDs. Communication messages that included posters, video spots, exhibition materials, etc. were developed vigorously to promote the use of condoms along with HIV prevention.

### *National AIDS Control Programme II*

National AIDS Control Programme **Phase-II (1999–2006)** was aimed at reducing the spread of HIV infection in India and strengthen India's capacity to respond to the HIV epidemic on a long-term basis. This phase can be called as health and reverse phase of the epidemic. Phase II also committed India to a dramatic 'paradigm shift' as insisted by the World Bank and allied donors. During this phase de-centralised state and municipal-level AIDS

Control Societies (SACS/MACS), as also registered societies functioning outside government control, assigning a pivotal position to NGOs in implementation and a focus on non-judgmental 'high impact prevention interventions targeting populations engaging in high risk behaviours' (Chhabra, 2007:105).

The policy and strategic shift was reflected in the two key objectives of NACP-II:

- to reduce the spread of HIV infection in India;
- to increase India's capacity to respond to HIV & AIDS on a long-term basis.

The primary aim of NACP-II was to keep HIV sero-prevalence low. Policy initiatives taken during NACP-II include: adoption of the National AIDS Prevention and Control Policy (2002); National Blood Policy; a strategy for Greater Involvement of People with HIV & AIDS (GIPA); launching of the National Rural Health Mission; launching of National Adolescent Education Programme; provision of anti-retroviral treatment (ART); formation of an inter-ministerial group for mainstreaming; and setting up of the National Council on AIDS, chaired by the Prime Minister (NACO, 2006:2).

NACP-II placed a greater emphasis on targeted interventions for high-risk groups, preventive interventions among the general population, and involvement of NGOs and other sectors and line departments, such as education, transport and police. Targeted interventions scaled up to cover a higher percentage of the population, and monitoring and evaluation was strengthened. In order to induce a sense of urgency, the classification of states was focused on the vulnerability of states. The states were classified as high and moderate prevalence (on the basis of HIV prevalence among high-risk and general population groups) and high and moderate vulnerability (on the basis of demographic characteristics of the population). The major challenges that remained were, in raising the overall effectiveness of state-level programs, expanding the participation of other sectors, increasing safe behaviour and reducing stigma associated with HIV-positive people among the population. With the growing complexity of the epidemic, changes were brought into policy frameworks and approaches of the NACP. Focus shifted from raising awareness to behaviour change. The National AIDS Prevention and Control Policy and the National Council on AIDS (NCA), chaired by the Prime Minister, provided policy guidelines for the epidemic. In November 1999, NACP-II was launched with financial credit support from the World Bank for Rs. 959 Crores. The Government of India allotted Rs. 196 Crores for this phase of the AIDS control programme. The final outlay from all sources was about Rs 2,064.65 Crores[4] for the NACP-II. The majority of the funding for the NACP-II came from the Department for International Development (DFID) (Rs. 487.4 Crores) followed by the USAID (Rs. 230.58 Crores). The contribution from the Global Fund was Rs. 122.74 Crores. The United Nations Development Programme (UNDP) funded the NACP-II for Rs. 6.47

Crores. Other international donors such as the Canadian International Development Organisation (CIDA) funded around Rs. 37.81 Crores whereas AusAID provided a funding for Rs. 24.65 Crores. All the organisations provided funding as well as technical assistance to the National AIDS Control Organisation (NACO). While the World Bank and DFID were the major donors, the Bill and Melinda Gates Foundation and the Global Fund for AIDS, TB and Malaria, have become increasingly important donors since 2004 for the HIV & AIDS control programme in India. The focus of NACP-II moved from the more diffuse goal of generating awareness on HIV prevention, to targeted intervention, a concept that was introduced in the latter part of NACP-I. The targeted intervention approach was meant to change high risk behaviour in populations who were at risk of contracting the infection and spreading it in the general population. NACP-II set up more than 1,000 targeted interventions, mostly through NGOs, for commercial sex workers, men having sex with men, injecting drug users, street children, prisoners, transgenders, truck drivers and migrant labour. NACP-II recruited local level people and trained them as peer educators to counsel, provide condoms through social marketing and provide information to encourage a change in behaviour (NACO, 2011). Some 845 clinics providing STD treatment were upgraded during NACP-II. NACP-II also contained a number of programmes directed at the general community. Mass education campaigns were conducted using print media, electronic media and folk-art forms, especially directed at people under the age of 25 years. Sex education programmes were introduced in schools, colleges and youth forums such as the National Service Scheme, Nehru Yuva Kendras and the Village Talk AIDS programme. By the end of the second phase of the programme, the number of licensed blood banks increased to 1,230 including 82 blood component separation centres. In addition to testing for HIV, blood banks were required to test all donated blood for Hepatitis C and an external quality assurance system for HIV testing was set up. HIV transmission through blood was reduced to less than 2% (from 8% when surveillance first started in the late 1980s) by the end of NACP-II. Voluntary Counselling and Testing Centres (VCTCs) were introduced early in NACP-II (NACO, 2004a). Counselling and testing enabled those at risk to know their HIV status and seek treatment, which was becoming available more widely. VCTCs also provided referrals to services for treatment and care. Services for the prevention of mother-to-child transmission of HIV, and for the provision of antiretroviral drugs to people with AIDS became linked to the VCTCs as and when these were instituted by the government. The Programme for Prevention of Mother (later Parent) to Child Transmission (PPTCT) of HIV aimed to prevent the transmission of HIV from pregnant, HIV-positive women to their children. This programme offered pregnant women testing for HIV and drugs and advice to those who were HIV-positive. Towards the end of the programme, PPTCT centres were combined with VCTCs to form Integrated Counselling and Testing Centres (ICTCs). Treatment and prophylaxis for opportunistic infections was an important strategy in NACP-II as the programme began to recognise the need to move beyond prevention and start providing medical services related to AIDS. For people with more advanced illness, the programme advocated the 'continuum of care' model with home-based care and hospital referral when appropriate, that was implemented through the NGOs. By the end of NACP-II, 122 community care centres (NACO, 2007), or hospices for the care of terminally ill AIDS patients were set up throughout the country. Around 2006, about 56,000 patients received first line antiretroviral drugs from 107 ART centres throughout the country (NACO, 2004b).

### National AIDS Control Programme III

National AIDS Control Programme **Phase-III (2007–12)** was based on the experiences and lessons drawn the earlier two phases. The overall goal of this phase was to 'halt and reverse' the HIV & AIDS epidemic in India. It intended to achieve this by integrating programmes for prevention, care, support and treatment. During this phase, Rs. 2,000 Crores was earmarked for a single prevention commodity—condoms (Chhabra, 2007). Sub-populations such as sex workers, men who have sex with men and injecting drug users were accorded highest priority in the intervention programme. At the same time long-distance truckers, prisoners, migrants (including refugees) and street children were next line on the basis of priority, that's because NACP-II had concentrated a lot on them. Treatment of STIs, access to prophylaxis and management of opportunistic infections and people who need access to ART were assured first line ARV (Antiretroviral) drugs. Universal provision of PPTCT services and access to pediatric Anti-Retroviral Therapy (ART) were prioritised. During this phase, enormous public resources were utilised to create organisations around sexual identity/practice. The aim of this approach was to persuade persons engaged in high-risk behaviours to go in for 'harm-minimising protection', i.e., through condoms, STD treatment, new needles. Thereby, the state becomes 'proactive for creating safe space' for commercial sex work and other high-risk situations (NACO, 2006).

### Objectives of NACP-III

The strategic objective of NACP-III (NACO, 2006: 5) was prevention of new infections in high-risk groups and the general population. The saturation of coverage of high-risk groups with Targeted Interventions (TIs) by scaled-up interventions in the general population was the primary objective. It also gave prominence to providing greater care, support and treatment to larger number of PLHA and further strengthening the infrastructure, systems and human resources in prevention, care, support and treatment programmes at the district, state and national level. This was to be complemented by strengthening the nationwide Strategic Information Management System. This phase was conspicuously silent on the structural socio-economic vulnerabilities and the root causes of the continuing flow of sub-populations into situations involving high-risk behaviour. In NACP-III, 1.3 million CSW; 1.3 million MSM; 190,000 IDU were mobilised and organised in groups (NACO, 2006: 193). The budget allocation was pre-occupied with getting high-risk groups to use condoms, besides 'addressing reduce vulnerabilities and break the silence surrounding issues related to sexuality'. (NACO, 2006: ii). The budgetary allocation for the NACP-III was Rs. 7,009 Crores[5]. The direct budgetary support from the government was for Rs. 2,861 Crores. The External Aid Component (EAC) was for Rs. 4,148 Crores. Much of the funding came from the World Bank in the External Aid Component (EAC). The World Bank allocated Rs. 1,328 Crores, which included $ 295 million USD including retroactive financing for 2006–7. GFATM (Round II, III and IV) financed around Rs. 824 Crores and the GFATM (Round VI) funded for Rs. 963 Crores for the NACP-III. The DFID funded Rs. 808 Crores (£ 95 million).

### National AIDS Control Programme IV

The funding for the NACP Phase IV was significantly reversed owing to economic recession and changing priorities of global NGOs. The Cabinet Committee on Economic Affairs (CCEA) approved a gross budgetary support of Rs 8,632.77 Crores for its implementation. NACP-IV is primarily aimed at accelerating the reversal process and ensuring integration of the programme response (Daily Pioneer, 2013). The funding pattern reversal impacted the financial burden of India which had to mitigate 76% of the financial burden on its own, with foreign donors pitching in the remaining 24%. This was in sharp contrast to the 75:25 pattern followed in the past wherein India had to take care of just the 25% while the international donors took care of the remainder. The total cost of Phase IV would be Rs. 11,394 Crores. The primary focus of Phase IV was on reducing infection and prevention of transmission of HIV & AIDS in the country. The main objective was to reduce new infections by 50% (2007 baseline of NACP-III) and provide comprehensive care and support to all persons living with HIV & AIDS, and treatment services to the needy. Funding agencies like the Global Fund to Fight AIDS, Tuberculosis and Malaria (The Global Fund), UK Department for International Development (DFID) and the Gates Foundation cut down their contributions to the India's AIDS control programme owing to various reasons. India had the highest caseload, with 2.5 million infections after Nigeria and South Africa. Though cases have reduced by over 50% over the last ten years, challenges remain (Bill & Melinda Gates Foundation, 2009).

Table 2.1 gives an overview on the three phases of the National AIDS Control Programme in India, which outlines the prominent strategies adopted to combat the epidemic. The table also ideates on the communication shifts and approaches during each phase. Prominent policies and frameworks during each phase have been indicated.

*Table 2.1* National AIDS Control Programme (I–IV) at a Glance

| Phase I (1992–99) | • Aimed at the general population with generic or clinical messages<br>• Fear-provoking images that led to AIDS phobia and stigma and discrimination of infected people at all levels<br>• National Blood Transfusion Policy was formulated<br>• Condoms are the only method with which HIV can be controlled<br>• Repositioning condom for STD prevention<br>• Control of STDs was an important strategy for HIV prevention<br>• NACP-I introduced the targeted intervention strategy |
|---|---|
| Phase II (1999–2006) | • Focus shifts from awareness generation to behaviour change<br>• Decentralised response and an increasing engagement of NGOs and networks of people living with HIV & AIDS<br>• Voluntary Counselling and Testing Centres (VCTCs) were introduced<br>• Services for the prevention of mother-to-child transmission of HIV, and for the provision of antiretroviral drugs to people with AIDS, became linked to the VCTCs as and when these were instituted by the government<br>• Moved beyond prevention and started providing medical services related to AIDS<br>• Institutionalisation of state-wide AIDS societies model<br>• Antiretroviral drugs were available in the market |
| Phase III (2007–12) | • Integrated package of prevention, care and support and treatment with the aim of reducing incidence<br>• Behaviour Change Communication approach strengthened by involving NGOs and various other philanthropic organisations |
| Phase IV (2013–17) | • Reduce new infections by 50% (2007 Baseline of NACP-III)<br>• Comprehensive care, support and treatment to all persons living with HIV & AIDS |

## Research design

The primary approach of the study was to gain insight on the social construction of sexual health in India through multiple methods of enquiry. The book carries out analysis of documents, posters and short films analysis that were accompanied /supplemented by in-depth and open-ended interviews along with a case study method. A comparative approach was employed while analysing the cases. This book attempts to understand the dynamics and the broader perspective that guide the approaches on sexual health in India. For which, it relies on a broad research approach and frequently uses open research questions to discover important categories, dimensions and inter-relationships for such analysis. An attempt was made to problematise/ operationalise the concepts that were the key to further investigations in the course of the research. Data collection and analysis proceeded concurrently throughout the study. The qualitative research done for this study can be understood as a complex system that was more than the sum of its parts. People were contacted directly, situations and phenomena were studied in order to gain insight on multiple interdependencies. Thick description, inquiry in depth and direct quotations capturing people's personal perspectives and experiences formed the qualitative data to describe how people were experiencing the phenomenon. The author's personal involvement in projects such as 'Developing Behaviour Change Communication material' for the various targeted interventions of the AIDS Control Society of Andhra Pradesh (APSACS) helped me a lot in understanding the dynamics of sexual health. The job involved working with the target groups, conducting group discussions, concept/field testing of the developed material on the target groups. Such exercises required extensive research on the lifestyles, study of the behaviours of the group, and their sexual activities as well. Other project experience like the Andhra Pradesh Health Systems Responsiveness Study (2001) funded by the WHO, Patients Satisfaction Survey and Hospital Performance Analysis funded by the World Bank further strengthened the methodologies employed in data collection. During these projects, I tried to understand the existing health systems, epidemiology of the people and the various approaches, policies and programmes that affected them directly or indirectly. Observations and insights formed an integral part of the inquiry and were critical in understanding the subject. Locking up in rigid designs that eliminate responsiveness was avoided, and the adoption of new paths of discoveries followed. In addition to this, the fieldwork involved collection of policy-related documents and interaction with resource persons in the allied areas of AIDS control both at the central level and state level as well as with the people from the advertising agencies. The theoretical premises guiding the research are Social Constructionism (Berger & Luckmann, 1966) and Bio-Power (Foucault, 1978). This book also attempts to probe into the role of the state in the construction of normative sexual health through communication campaigns. It also seeks to examine the background, understanding of the professionals involved at each level, and how grounded are their perception of sexual health vis-à-vis the actual realities. In this work, I also seek to understand the sexual health campaigns through the perspective of a social constructionist perspective and analyse how the 'task of communicating sexual health' has been 'owned' by the state. I apply a critical stance to interrogate the discourses adopted in sexual health campaign messages in India, with the ultimate goal of using the criticism for creating a constitutive space that encourages the articulation, comparison and synthesis of alternative approaches to health communication campaigns. The study will also help in understanding the process through which the meanings of sexual health is constructed and negotiated for the development of scholarship on health communication, which gets translated into posters and messages to be disseminated all over the country. The study seeks to contribute to the existing literature on sexual health communication through an understanding of the communicative struggles of a marginalised community. The specific objectives of this study are to trace the growth and evolution of the concept of sexual health from a health communication policy perspective and understand the role of the state in determining the form and structure of sexual health time to time. It also tries to carry out a comparative analysis of the sexual health communication policies/approaches of different countries to further understand and evolve a common framework for learnings for India. Prominently, the book tries to study and understand the dominant approaches adopted for the sexual health communication campaigns from 1997–2012 with the backdrop of HIV & AIDS.

### Comparative analysis

Studying and comparing cases helps uncover the dynamics of the HIV & AIDS programme. It also seeks to investigate why certain things work well in some situations and fail in others. Six countries, four developing and two developed countries were chosen for the study. These countries were selected based on UNAIDS country-wise HIV & AIDS prevalence ranking given on their website. These countries were analytically connected through a common framework arrived through coding. Common themes that identify consequential features and patterns across various countries were explored. The comparative method was employed to study the international policy perspectives. Such comparative analysis helped to study the international policy perspectives on sexual health and communication strategies. Cross-national comparisons contribute to the area of HIV & AIDS policy as a means of evaluating the solutions adopted for dealing with problems that are common among different countries. It is also important, however, to take into account the political structures and the historical and religious context within which such policies are adopted in a particular country.

### Document analysis

Document analysis helps in understanding the process, context and meaning of a situation or social activity (Altheide, 1996) and consists of extensive reading, sorting and searching through the material to make comparisons on the basis of categories and concepts through coding (described in the coding and data analysis section). Document analysis of official publications, factual records, reports and declarations allowed for a historical study of health campaigns promoting sexual health with a particular reference to population control as well as HIV & AIDS. The documents also helped further in understanding the operations and legislative framework of health policies in India. Analysis of documents released by organisations involved in HIV & AIDS, population control helped in tracing the ideology behind them and the course of policy formulations undertaken. In addition, audio material, websites of organisations and postings on the HIV & AIDS email list servers were also examined. The purpose of the document analysis was also to understand the making of public policies for tackling a problematic social issue and analyse the government strategies about the HIV & AIDS issue. Through document analysis, I have tried to identify the stakeholders and actors involved in those processes, their positions, the powers, the networks and their strategies, as well as the government strategies.

### Poster and short films analysis

Roland Barthes (1977) classifies three distinct but related parts of a visual communication system: a linguistic message, a coded iconic message and a non-coded iconic message. Because images are 'polysemous' and are open to multiple meanings, he argues that the text is used to 'fix the floating chain of signifieds' and give the image its meaning. In this way, the verbal message has traditionally dominated the visual sign. The visual component can also be seen as 'an independently organised and structured message—connected with the verbal text, but in no way dependent on it' (Kress and van Leeuwen, 2001). According to them, there are three meta-functions: the ideational, which refers to how objects are represented in an image and how they interact with one another; the interpersonal, which refers to the relationship among the producer, the receiver and the image; and the textual, which refers to the composition of the image. Various other theorists see visual communications and language as socially constructed and culturally determined. In this part of the analysis, attempts were made to understand how language has been used in messages, its inherent meanings and underlying demeanour was ana-lysed. Images on kinds of people shown, social/cultural background depicted and the representation of gender were also analysed.

### In-depth and open-ended interviews

Qualitative methods such as in-depth interviews are better suited than quan-titative methods to explore and study meanings, experiences and social con-struction processes. They provide the participant an opportunity to account for their understanding in their own words, and to account for their perception of reality as constructed by society on sexual health reflects in their under-standing. These methods are consistent with both social constructionism and bio-power perspectives. The research design that was used in this study was an interview. Interviews served as an opportunity to further discuss questions that would emerge from their own accounts. In this way, the participants were able to define their own reality, to define their perceptions of normative sexual health perceptions as they felt best and in this way had their voices heard in the research account. Attempts were made to contact the participants six months after the last interview to discuss some of the preliminary findings with them. This opportunity provided confirmation and feedback from some of the participants and provided them with an opportunity to be part of the research process and the creation of knowledge. It also provided an assessment of participants' feelings and experiences, their feedback regarding the research process, and shall also provide them with an account of the ways in which the process has enlightened and changed the study. Mies (1983) indicated that in order for knowledge to be non-oppressive, it has to emerge through dialogue rather than one-side questioning. By using the proposed methodology, I attempted to make this research process as non-oppressive and non-hierarchical as possible by including participants as collaborators and co-creators of the knowledge creation process (Villanueva, 1997).

### Case study method

Case studies bring out the details of an individual, group, organisation or event by using multiple sources of data (Wimmer and Dominick, 1987) and are an ideal methodology when a holistic, in-depth investigation is needed. A case study is a multi-perspective analysis that 'investigates a contemporary phenomenon within its real-life context, especially when the boundaries between the phenomenon and context are not clearly evident' (Yin 2003:13). Yin also stresses the need for generalisations and describes case studies as an occasional early step in theory building (Stake, 1995; Denzin, 1989).

A pilot study was also carried out. Two persons from the National AIDS Control Organisation (NACO) were interviewed at New Delhi. One was part of NACP-I in its initial years. Three other interviews were conducted in Hyderabad, Andhra Pradesh. One person was part of the team that developed a campaign in Andhra Pradesh on condom promotion called 'Do you have it?' One interview was conducted with a deputy chief executive of a reputable NGO, which had developed innovative campaigns for AIDS awareness in Andhra Pradesh. The results of the pilot study helped in making changes in the data collection techniques. It also provided feedback on the guidelines in analysis. In order for qualitative research to be valid, it should accurately depict the participant's experiences without trying to predict anything further. Also, it should portray a picture of the socio-cultural context around the experience. All the interviews were transcribed verbatim. This ascertained that all transcripts were true to their original sources and would give a feel of the data. The anthropological approach to research points out that in order for a researcher to understand a phenomenon in a given culture, the culture needs to be understood first; and that in order for a researcher to understand people, their language needs to be understood also. The author can act both as an 'insider' and as an 'outsider' to the culture. Since data for the study was collected in both English and Hindi languages, the participants had an opportunity to express themselves without the possibility of being misunderstood, or without the danger of not finding the appropriate words in English to express their feelings and meanings about normative sexual health. All the results and discussion have been analysed through the theoretical lenses of social constructionism and bio-power.

## Data collection procedures

*Collection of documents*

Documents pertaining to HIV & AIDS were collected from various sources. Extensive library research was carried out at the National AIDS Control Organisation (NACO) in New Delhi, the Indian Institute of Mass Communication, department library at the Social and Preventive Medicine at the Jawaharlal Nehru University, Department of Anthropology, Delhi University and at the National Institute of Health and Family Welfare (NIHFW) at New Delhi and Hyderabad. Declarations, standing committee reports, etc. relating to sexual health i.e., population control and HIV & AIDS were collected. The World Health Organisation (WHO), UNAIDS, World Bank and IMF websites were search extensively to collect information on the policy documents on HIV & AIDS. Please see Appendix I for declarations referred to in this study.

*Collection of posters and films*

Posters were collected from the National AIDS Control Organisation's (NACO) office in New Delhi. NACO has painstakingly collected the Information, Education and Communication (IEC) material it has developed and has put it on its website (www.nacoonline.org). These posters have been arranged under various themes. The IEC material can be downloaded from the site. 165 posters were downloaded from this site, 21 cartoon strips which were developed by it were also downloaded. These strips contained stories related to risk behaviour under various circumstances. 35 video spots developed by NACO were also collected from NACO office in New Delhi and from its website. The primary focus of the research is to understand how the state has got involved in socially constructing the sexual health messages for the masses in India. Therefore, only those posters that had the NACO logo on them were classified for further analysis. These posters were again organised into various categories which evolved based on the Polgar's models of social construction discussed in Chapter 6. Several posters fell into multiple categories. Therefore, they were carefully looked into and later on categorised based on themes that were evolving as the analysis progressed. Data collection and analysis was a continuous process. Finally, 73 posters (one poster has been used for two different contexts) and 22 short films were analysed for the study. Twenty-six posters were also collected on Balbir Pasha Campaign from the Population Services International (PSI) office in Hyderabad/ Delhi and few of them were sourced from the internet. Eleven video spots were also collected from the offices of PSI. The PSI also runs a dedicated website on Balbir Pasha Campaign (www.balbirpasha.in). Posters and video spots were also collected on the Bindaas Bol, BBC World Service Trust campaign from the offices of NACO and from the internet.

### In-depth and open-ended interviews

Twelve participants at their workplaces/residences in New Delhi, Trivandrum, Hyderabad and Chennai were contacted and a time was set to meet in person for the discussion of the study requirements. The interview date and time was selected usually within one to two weeks after having sent an interview guide (see Appendix 2). They were instructed to express about their understanding of sexual health in terms of three major areas: (a) the sources of sexual messages, (b) the incidence and effect of any type of sexual experience in their sexual definitions and (c) the influence that these messages, along with their past experiences, have had on the ways in which they receive sexual health messages. The probes used to elicit more information from the participant were based only on the information already presented. The interviews were held in the participant's site of preference allowing them to have choice and privacy (Kimmel & Moody, 1990; Strain & Chappell, 1982). Most of the time, the interviews took place at the participant's site of work or at their residences. I requested the consent of participants to audiotape the interviews for further analysis. As the last step, I attempted to contact all participants six months later for an individual meeting or phone conversation. In this conversation I presented the individuals with preliminary findings and interpretations of their interviews. The main purpose of this interview was to seek confirmation and feedback regarding the interpretations of the data provided. While I was not able to contact all participants, the feedback from those contacted is presented as part of the discussion. By including this step, participants had an opportunity to contribute and be part of the research process (Baber & Allen, 1992; Thompson, 1992).

### Case studies

*Bindaas Bol, Balbir Pasha, Men can make a difference* and *What kind of a man are you?*—are the four campaigns that were selected after consultations and thorough review of literature. While building a separate argument on the social construction of masculinity, the discourse on condom was very prominent. Therefore, these cases, which specifically aimed at men and their risk behaviours were chosen. The material for these four campaigns was collected from the internet, NACO headquarters in New Delhi and various other NGOs in Andhra Pradesh and Delhi.

### Coding and data analysis

The content of the posters, short films, in-depth interviews, feedback on interpretations and personal notes were considered as data in the analysis. The qualitative data analysis techniques used in this study involved a combination of those described by Bogdan and Biklen (1982), Strauss and Corbin (1990) and Taylor and Bogdan (1984). The analysis was based on the theoretical perspectives that guided the study (social construction and concepts of bio-power), the participants' own accounts and discussions regarding their constructions of sexuality, and their own understanding. Whereas Strauss and Corbin (1990) advocate a parallel and ongoing collection and analysis of the data, Bogdan and Biklen (1982) suggest that only experienced researchers in qualitative studies are able to accomplish this effectively and efficiently. Although it was inevitable that some reflection on the content of the narratives and the interviews occurred during the data gathering process (Bogdan & Biklen, 1982), the formal analysis of the data started after all data were collected (Allen et al., 1989). Taylor and Bogdan (1984:130) divide the analysis process in three stages: (a) 'Identifying themes and developing concepts', (b) 'Coding the data and refining one's understanding of the subject matter' and (c) 'Understanding the data in the context in which they were collected'. My analysis of the data addressed these as follows. The posters were coded into various categories based on the models suggested by Polgar (1996). Written narratives and audiotaped interviews were transcribed. This step provided an early exposure to the data and helped familiarise the themes that were evolving. Through repeated careful readings of the data, emerging themes, concepts and theoretical propositions were obtained (Taylor & Bogdan, 1984:130–33). The coding of emerging themes was guided by the systematic outline described by Bogdan and Biklen and an adaptation of Strauss and Corbin (1990:61) open and axial coding. Open coding is 'the process of breaking down, examining, comparing, conceptualizing, and categorizing data'. Axial coding refers to a set of procedures used to put data back together in different ways after open coding by making connections between categories (Strauss & Corbin, 1996:96). The list of emerging themes was fairly large, axial coding began before open coding of all data was completed. I attempted to re-arrange, combine and redefine categories to fit the data. Taylor and Bogdan (1984:137) point out that the goal of coding is to make the codes fit the data and not the data fit the codes, therefore coding included refining the coding scheme, adding categories, collapsing them and redefining the categories. The context in which the interviews were collected, my own recorded comments, assumptions and theoretical memos were also considered in the analysis. As much as possible, preliminary interpretations of findings were shared with several participants either by phone or in person for them to review and react to. Qualitative methodology was employed for accomplishing the objectives of this study. Qualitative approach provides an insight on the social construction of sexual health in India through multiple methods of enquiry. A thorough analysis of policy documents, posters and short films analysis were accompanied/supplemented by in-depth and open-ended interviews along with the case study method. Whilst analysing cases, a comparative approach was employed. The theoretical premises guiding the research are social constructionism (Berger & Luckmann, 1966) and bio-power (Foucault, 1979). This broader objective of this study is to understand the dynamics and the broader perspective that guide the approaches on sexual health in India. For which, the study relied on a broad research approach and frequently used open research questions to discover important categories, dimensions and inter-relationships for such analysis. The qualitative research done for this study can be understood as a complex system that was more than the sum of its parts. Posters along with document analysis preceded the interviews to gain insight on multiple interdependencies. Thick description of posters as well as documents were associated with direct quotations from the interviews. This study applies such critical stance to interrogate the discourses adopted in sexual health campaigns messages in India, with the ultimate goal of using the criticism for creating a constitutive space that encourages the articulation, comparison and synthesis of alternative approaches to health communication campaigns. The study also helps in understanding the process through which the meanings of sexual health is constructed and negotiated for the development of scholarship on health communication, which gets translated into posters and messages to be disseminated all over the country. The study seeks to contribute to the existing literature on sexual health communication through an understanding of the communicative struggles of a marginalised community. The specific objectives of this study are to trace the growth and evolution of the concept of sexual health from a health communication policy perspective and understand the role of the state in determining the form and structure of sexual health. The study also is a comparative analysis of the sexual health communication policies/approaches of different countries to further understand and evolve a common framework of learnings for India which would give an overall purview of the dominant approaches adopted for the sexual health communication campaigns from 1997–2012 in the backdrop of HIV & AIDS epidemic. The study attempted to seek answers on how social and institutional sources influence the ways in which normative sexual health messages are developed and delivered to a wider audience. Moreover, it also wanted to know how personal beliefs and perceptions influence the process of developing sexual health messages in a multicultural country like India. And asks: How are sexual health messages created, changed and modified as part of social discourse by the institutions that develop sexual health messages?

## Overview of book

The book contains six chapters including the introductory chapter and the concluding chapter, Chapter 6, on the social construction of sexual citizenship. Chapter 1 provides a broad overview of the concepts of sexual health and communication approaches in India. Chapter 1 also explains the conceptual framework of the study and explains in detail the research strategy and methodology adopted for the study and outlines the critical questions, issues and discourses related to sexual health and HIV & AIDS that are addressed comprehensively to examine the contextualisation of sexual health in India. Chapter 2 also traces the historical evolution and politics of sexual health in India. Parallels have been drawn between the population control programme and the HIV & AIDS programme in India. It further elucidates the similarity in its agenda. A historic approach of understanding HIV & AIDS in India, its growth, programme, various policy initiatives and attempts to probe how the discourse on sexual health has got institutionalised has also been undertaken. Chapter 3 illustrates and delves into a comparative analysis of sexual health policies around the world. Chapter 3 looks into the sexual health policies of developed countries which have the distinction of excellent track records. Sexual health policies of countries such as Uganda, Lesotho, Thailand and Swaziland have also been analysed. Uganda has often been quoted as a country with the best track record of containing the HIV & AIDS and thus improving the sexual health of its citizens. Lessons have been drawn from this analysis for India. Chapter 4 and Chapter 5 are thematic and give an overview of the empirical observations and analyses the findings of the various sexual health messages and policies. Chapter 5 deals exhaustively with the aspect of the condom and debates its vigorous re-introduction into the Indian society as a tool for sexual health control.

## Notes

1 The 1857 mutiny is usually dubbed as the 'First Indian War of Independence' or as a 'Sepoy Mutiny'. It was a mass mutiny by a garrison of native Indian Sepoys (soldiers) of the British East India Company. Hard and violent battles were fought for 15 months and finally the British East India Company was able to quell the mutiny using advanced western arms and ammunition and a far better organised army.
2 http://digital.nls.uk/indiapapers/institutions.html accessed on 12/01/2013.
3 www.colby.edu/personal/t/thtieten/Famplan.htm#_ftn5 accessed on 18/01/2011.
4 http://naco.gov.in/about-us/funds-and-expenditures-0 accessed on 13/07/2017.
5 http://naco.gov.in/about-us/funds-and-expenditures-0 accessed on 13/07/2017.

# 3 Sexual health communication

## Mainstreaming taboos and mediating social construction

What is the sexual health understanding in India? How do discourses of sexual health messages affect targeted population whilst influencing their behaviour? How has the term 'sexual health' through the HIV & AIDS epidemic become accultured into India? This chapter attempts to seek answers to such questions. This chapter discusses the theoretical framework of the concepts that guided this study. A brief overview on the social constructions of sexual health have been discussed. It also delves into the evolution of sexual health approaches worldwide that includes population control programmes. Based on which, a parallel has been drawn between the agendas of population control and HIV & AIDS. Going back to history of independent India, it can be inferred that population control was a major attempt by the Government of India to stake control over the sexual health. This chapter ends with a discussion on the major approaches adopted to analyse the HIV & AIDS messages in India.

'Human Immunodeficiency Virus (HIV) that causes Acquired Immune Deficiency Syndrome (AIDS) has no cure or vaccine, but can only be tackled with education directed at changing behaviours' (Sibthorpe, 1992: 255). The global understanding of the transmission of virus is that it is largely caused by sexual behaviours (deviant) worldwide necessitating a global definition of sexual health as a basis for prevention and care. The WHO definition does not seem adequate and relevant everywhere for a worldwide adoption. Local adoption of the concept of sexual health requires knowledge of history and culture of a particular society and will always be strongly determined by specific social conditions, including religious and cultural values, as well as the category of people—in terms of age, gender, ethnicity, sexual orientation etc. and its intersections—one is dealing with. It has been observed in various contexts that the actual operationalisation of sexual health in policy documents varies and is affected by a variety of factors, including political and economic circumstances. In spite of all the caveats of cultural diversity that impact notions of sexual health, a clearly stated concept of sexual health may be useful, because such a concept offers a framework for thinking about goals to be accomplished, and issues to be explored. Thereby, transmission of HIV & AIDS messages by the Government of India is by and large influenced by the cultural and political factors.

## Social construction theory—theorising sexual health

Social construction theory is broadly understood as, how individuals perceive social reality based on their own experiences and contributes to knowledge creation (Berger & Luckmann, 1966). Hoffman (1990) suggests that this knowledge gets constructed through social interpretation and inter-subjective influence of language, family, and culture. As a result of which, this conceptual framework further emphasises the cultural and historical aspects of phenomena that is understood to be natural that eventually develops through interaction in the social context (Conrad & Barker, 2010:67). At the same time, any person's conception of reality about fear, danger, and stigma is very individualistic, but this kind of perception is largely influenced by cultural patterns (Ferrante, 1988:22). This perspective of reality and understanding about an event, actions, attitudes, and beliefs are majorly mediated by historical and cultural factors. Social constructionist inquiry is principally concerned with explicating the process by which people come to describe, explain, or otherwise account for the world (including themselves) in which they live (Gergen, 1985:266). In social constructionism, basic understanding of reality is also determined by the available concepts, categories, and methods. These concepts incline the researcher to certain lines of enquiry where the results are the products more of our languages than of empirical discovery (Villanueva, 1997). Any individual's active role in construction of reality is guided by her/his culture (Tiefer, 1987, 1995 as cited in Villanueva, 1997). They construct knowledge based on the prevalent discourses about certain issues in their lives, societies, and cultures. In the context of HIV & AIDS, physically identical sexual acts may have different social and personal meanings depending on how they are defined and understood in their different cultures and historical periods. Besides influencing the way individuals define and act on their behaviours, socio-historical constructions also organise and give meaning to collective sexual experience through, for instance, constructions of sexual identities, definitions, ideologies, and regulations (Vance, 1991 as cited in Villanueva, 1997).

While sex is biologically determined, sexual behaviour is under social control. It is regulated by cultural constructs that identify the appropriate persons and circumstances with which and in which sexuality may be expressed. Regulation thus imbues sexual behaviour with social meaning by reinforcing and controlling the terms and conditions of interpersonal relationships and procreation (Sibthorpe, 1992). HIV & AIDS is also a very complex disease because of the body of knowledge it has generated ever since it started. Huber & Gillapsy (1998:191) state that the body of knowledge associated with HIV & AIDS represents a complexity not present in any other disease. Furthermore, the epidemic has altered the model of information production and consumption and has spawned its own vernacular, one representative of a diverse population of information producers and consumers. HIV & AIDS as a chronic disease that gets shaped by various domains that include political, social, economic, legal, philosophical, psychological, religious, and spiritual ramifications associated with the illness. Such kinds of societal construct within which the body of knowledge concerning HIV & AIDS exists mirrors the complexities of the malady and the various controversies associated with it (Huber & Gillapsy, 1998). As stated earlier, constructing the sexual health as a social problem requires a subjective evaluation. An 'objective' analysis of the problem would diverge widely and state how the problem is perceived by different sections of the society. Blumer (1971) points out that sociological recognition of a social problem is usually preceded by its designation as a problem by the public. Therefore, sexual health can be studied in either 'objective' or the 'subjective' way. Spector & Kitsuse (1977) as cited in Pavarala (1996), treat social problems as social constructions that are created and maintained through expression of claims about social reality by individuals and groups, and subsequent responses of others. Therefore, out of such interaction grows institutionalisation. Society as a set of institutions confronts the individual as a given objective reality and each person is socialised into perceiving it as a given fact. While reality is socially defined, definitions of it are embodied in concrete individuals and groups who do the defining. The multiple ways of understanding a given reality, which is rooted in specific frames of reference or orientation, is said to be role specific (Holzner, 1968). Following this line of thought this chapter seeks to determine interpretations of 'health' based on the fact that it is a very dynamic and interdisciplinary field, evidenced by an attempt to understand the human experience, past and present. Such an understanding of health and the 'multiple realities' of experiencing health will provide vital information critical to interpreting health behaviour. Culture here is conceptualised as both transformative and constitutive, providing an axis for theorising the discursive, processed through which meanings are socially constructed by members. This process is considered to be a dialectical one. Stressing the 'relational, processual, and contradictory nature of knowledge production' (Martin & Nakayama, 1999:14), the dialectical approach captures the meaning construction as a dynamic cultural process, with the possibility of coexistence of multiple, and often contradictory, meanings. The objective is to develop an understanding of the complexity of meanings constructed around health rather than drawing neatly packaged stable constructs that might inform one-way campaigns of health communication. The conceptualisation of an invitational rhetoric as an alternative to the dominant persuasion rhetoric, the culture-centred approach to health communication foregrounds the voices of marginalised people, in dialogue with the academic researcher or theorist, with the goals of developing mutual understanding and respect, as opposed to the imposing dominant world view (Foss & Griffin, 1995).

Social construction of sexual health is related to the values and norms about sexuality and health that come from a variety of sources including social and religious viewpoints, science, medicine, and individual experience. No single definition of sexual health will fully represent this diversity, at least in India. Indeed, a review of the emergence of the concept of sexual health concluded that there is no international consensus on the concept of sexual health and its implementation in public health policies (Giami 2002). This aspect has been detailed in later sections which attempt to analyse the sexual health policies of a few select developed as well as developing countries. Individuals or groups that suggest a particular definition of sexual health are likely to appear to have good reasons for their selection. However, these reasons are often informed by cultural practices that, as a result, produce a definition that uncritically fits the existing society. In this context it has been argued that it will not be possible to step outside of these cultural processes to develop a universally applicable concept of sexuality (Naus & Theis, 1991) and acknowledges that the same is true for the concept of sexual health. From the constructionist position the process of understanding is not automatically driven by the forces of nature, but is the result of an active, cooperative enterprise of persons in relationship. In this light, inquiry is invited into the historical and cultural bases of various forms of world construction (Gergen, 1985:267). This book tries to explore the cultural, societal, and personal normative sexual health messages that are socially constructed by the state through its institutions in India. It is appropriate to trace the evolution of sexual health messages historically looking at each institution that had developed over a period of time to address a particular issue of sexual health viz., population control, HIV & AIDS etc. (Hacker, 2002). Furthermore, historical institutionalism helps us understand not just *which* decisions were taken, but also *when* those particular decisions were taken along a policy path by paying heed to the *process* (timing and sequence) of politics and policymaking within given institutional parameters. This book also explores the manner in which various institutions 'educating the masses on sexual health' have evolved, shaped, and constructed their own meanings of sexual health and safe sex practices, and have developed their own sexual scripts, the ways in which sexual scripts and meanings influence their behaviour, and how sexual beliefs/perceptions determine the evolution of sexual scripts. The book also tries to explore how these perceptions influence their meanings and behaviours related to sexual health. It also tries to understand how sexual health messages are formed, how they are reconstructed through an individual's life, and how they influence the way institutions construct and experience their own normative sexual health definitions and practices.

In this work, a critical stance is applied to interrogate the communication approaches adopted in sexual health campaigns in India, with the ultimate goal of using the critique for creating a constitutive space that encourages the articulation, comparison, and synthesis of alternative approaches to health communication campaigns.

## Sexual health: The politics of international health concerns

Population programmes in India, were vertically designed—'top down' and bureaucratic in its shapes and implementation. The programmes are still designed, financed, controlled, and monitored from New Delhi. It could not become a 'people's movement' (Bose, 1998:135). The same holds true for HIV & AIDS as well. The National Health Policy (2002), National AIDS Prevention & Control (2003) and the National Blood Policy (2003) discuss the prevention mechanism to be carried among the poor and marginalised sections of the community who are at the highest of risk (NACO, 2004). The affected and the at-risk population were classified as the 'Targeted Interventions' and the rest of the population was called 'General Population'. The use of such 'disassociating' language (which can be formal or technical rather than, or as well as literally foreign) is found magnified in health ministries and organisations involved in sexual health promotion and disease prevention. In these settings, staff and other participants tend to become rapidly acculturated into using the international vocabulary of sexual health that includes phrases such as 'high risk' and a proliferation of acronyms such as STI (Sexually Transmitted Infection), MSM (Men who have Sex with Men) and CSW (Commercial Sex Worker).This phenomenon in turn has important implications for the mapping of local terms and understandings onto these putatively 'neutral' terminologies, since inevitably the use of these terms also imposes their category referents.

In a country like India, which is multilingual and multicultural, the language that discusses sex and sexuality evolves in different forms. HIV & AIDS field workers use the jargons from internationally (Western) developed vocabulary on sexual health extensively, to deter themselves from local discourses. A new (and potentially exclusionary) language and community gets created in the process. This commensurate implication for local identification with newly created and disseminated identity categories (Lambert, 2001; Foreman, 2004). Rather than utilising and building on local discourses of sexual health, a new language is being developed. Communication using language derived out of, and modified from, existing local parlance about sexual health (as locally understood) may be less potentially exclusionary and more effective in developing new knowledge, than that which uses language rooted in international health vocabulary. The language of sexual health used by international and local health agencies takes a highly particular, essentially biomedical form that may have no precise local referents. Thus, utilising local discourses that draw on indigenous definitions of health, which incorporate concerns with sexual regulation and propriety, to understand how sex and sexuality are locally conceived and to promote HIV preventive strategies, may be more fruitful than a direct focus on verbal renderings of these later constructs (Lambert & Wood, 2005). The potentially distorting and stigmatising consequences of attributing any aspect of the transmission of a virus to 'cultural factors' that have been documented, when this narrowly cultural approach is translated into HIV prevention interventions, it is often manifested in attempts to match the presentation—to 'look and sound'—of the intervention to the target population, and in attempts to address locally relevant themes within the intervention's content (Wilson & Miller, 2003).

However, these strategies are not informed by and do not address the cultural and structural *contexts* in which people live their sexual lives. Political economy and structural conditions as well as the socio-cultural milieu have a dynamics of socio-medical crises such as HIV & AIDS (Parker, 2000; Kalipeni et al., 2004). The many educational interventions that are based primarily on individual and social normative approaches—such as changing awareness and consciousness, improving communication skills, and shifting group norms—may not succeed on a major scale, even if appropriately tailored to local cultural assumptions, if they neglect the underlying dimensions of sexual ill-health. It was argued that nations that controlled their population problem will be better able to manage their resources and citizens and would provide the recipe for a global climate. Population control serves transnational hegemony by fostering conditions for sustainable development, which in turn promotes economic growth and new opportunities for businesses. Population control programmes embody other ideological biases that underlie the conceptualisation. The attention has shifted onto serving the status quo by focusing on individual-level behaviour change among the subaltern classes, those undesirable groups whose vastly growing masses need to be managed and controlled (Dutta, 2006). By focusing on population as the solution to problems of global peace and stability, the funding agencies and interventionists privilege national and international elite positions, minimising and shifting attention from the possibilities of real change in the condition of subalternity produced by practices of marginalisation and supporting the positions of elite privilege (Dutta-Bergmann, 2004).

## Population control and HIV & AIDS: Politics of sexual health

India has witnessed momentous and multidimensional changes in the arena of sexual and reproductive health in the last few decades. The policy and programme environment has undergone a significant shift from a family planning (control) approach to a broader orientation that stresses on sexual and reproductive health and the exercise of reproductive rights more comprehensively owing to the 'global catastrophe' of HIV & AIDS. While over the course of the 1990s, several studies have addressed aspects of sexual and reproductive health in India, there remains a need to synthesise the lessons learned, identify achievements and obstacles, and outline strategies and actions to enhance sexual and reproductive health in the twenty-first century. As the HIV & AIDS epidemic completes around 25 years of its existence in India and elsewhere, much of the sense of urgency that accompanied discussions of AIDS only ten or 15 years ago seem to be disappearing (Parker, 2000). Industrialised or developed countries have been able to make HIV & AIDS a manageable health condition due to the advent of new antiretroviral drugs. Few of the privileged 'developing' countries have also benefitted from the drugs (Parker, 2002). HIV & AIDS still continues to rage almost exclusively in the most marginalised sectors of the society regardless of the degree of development. These are the people who live in situations that are characterised by diverse forms of structural violence (Farmer, Connors, & Simmons, 1996 as cited in Parker, 2002). HIV as an epidemic continues in such kinds of spaces of poverty, gender inequality, and sexual oppression largely unaddressed by the formal public health and education programmes. 'HIV & AIDS in a way is also responsible for the growing polarisations between the very rich and the very poor thereby isolating some segments of the population' (Parker, 2002:344). Asish Bose (1998) in his book *From Population to People* states very categorically that no new ideas would emerge unless there is a sustained research by people of who have competence, integrity, and vision. There must be a continuous dialogue with the rural masses in which there is communication that respects human dignity and the sanctity of marriage and family and does not treat human beings as 'targets' for population control.

### The politics of controlling sexual health

Major funding agencies in the last one and a half decades have become lead 'development' agencies around the world who have taken upon themselves for the global response to HIV & AIDS (Parker, 2002). The World Development Report, 1993, titled *Investing in Health* was crucial in the perspective of the new economic order that was envisaged by it. The report replaced the term 'primary health care' with 'essential and clinical services', omitted communicable diseases from the category of essential public health activities and outlined the treatment of diabetes, cardiovascular diseases, cataracts, schizophrenia, etc. as priorities for the governments. Critics have regularly characterised these as attempts to provide healthcare to an exclusive class. Interestingly countries like India followed these directives *in toto*, in the form of budget cuts, formulating a new drug policy with decontrols and privatisation of medical care to name a few. This World Bank approach came to be known as 'health sector reforms' (Goswami, 2007:11). It has been criticised as being driven by economic and political ideology. Since, the early 1990s, in part as a response to critics who called attention to the frequently negative consequences of structural adjustment programme promoted by the World Bank together with the International Monetary Fund (IMF) has increasingly focussed on health-related issues, opening up new lending programmes and expanding the resources available for projects focusing on population, nutrition and similar issues throughout the developing world. (Parker, 2002:344). The interest of the multilateral, funding organisations and the international bodies can be traced to the times when population control was the prime concern. That was when population control was largely perceived through Western eyes, and the developing countries depended largely on the technical expertise of the Western world. India's family planning as well as the HIV & AIDS campaigns has been heavily influenced by foreign funding agencies and foreign experts of doubtful caliber. This has been counterproductive (Bose,

1998). The multinational corporations, the multi-institutions of global economic governance and the G8 group are the most dominant drivers of globalisation around the world. As a result of which, they also structure not only the contours of the epidemic in terms of transmission and new infections, but also the outcomes once an individual is sick with complications of HIV infection through their influence on patterns of 'labour mobility, economic performance and resilience, investment in healthcare services and education and even their influence on the moral economies of the developing world, but also the outcomes once an individual is sick with complications of HIV infection' (Boesten & Poku, 2009:6).

Matthew Connelly (2009) in his book *Fatal Misconception: The Struggle to Control World Population* explains how eugenics united some of the richest and most powerful elites of the twentieth century into a movement 'to remake humanity by controlling the population of the world,' answering to no one and bringing untold misery upon the world's poor. In 1952, at a secret, invitation-only gathering in Colonial Williamsburg, Virginia, John D. Rockefeller III brought together what would become the modern population control establishment. Setting the agenda for the following decades were the heads of the US Atomic Energy Commission and National Academy of Sciences, and top scientists 'from embryology to economics', including past and present Nobel Prize winners (Yoshihara, 2009:3).

Western countries decided radical measures to reduce birth rates after the genesis of Population Council, which went onto become the nexus of the entire population control movement around the world. It coordinated its work with United Nations, the Ford, and Rockefeller foundations, the International Planned Parenthood Federation (IPPF) as well as major pharmaceutical firms. The Population Control Programme adopted by India in 1952 allowed them to start experimenting on its people to find a cheap contraceptive. Most of the contraceptives were used in poverty-stricken slums and among the most ignorant people. These included such 'shock attacks' as quotas for millions of shoddy vasectomies and IUD insertions without follow-up care, public humiliation of poor families with three or more children, bulldozing of entire neighbourhoods, which displaced countless thousands of the poor and the known unloading of defective IUDs that crippled poor women (Yoshihara, 2009:4). One can draw parallel between the Population Control Programme and the HIV & AIDS programme in India. Both the programmes have much in common i.e., setting of 'targets', centralised 'blanket' approach, obsession with numbers, bureaucracy, rewards and punishments in the campaigns, which have been discussed later.

### *Models of social construction of sexual health through HIV & AIDS campaigns*

Social constructionism is a conceptual framework that 'emphasises the cultural and historical aspects of phenomena widely thought to be exclusively natural. The emphasis is on how meanings of phenomena do not necessarily themselves develop through interaction in a social context' (Conrad & Barker, 2010:67). Social constructionism examines how individuals and groups contribute to producing perceived social reality and knowledge (Berger & Luckmann, 1966). In the context of HIV & AIDS, the social construction specifically refers to several themes: the cultural meaning of HIV & AIDS as an illness that is not derived from the nature of the disease and that shapes the society's response to the afflicted people; the illness experience as constructed in the interplay of various social factors, which also refers to how people understand and communicate their illness in the daily context; and the medical knowledge as constructed and developed by the policy interests. The study broadly covers these themes of social construction of HIV & AIDS. Martin Levine (1992) examined the implications of constructionist theory on the epidemic by studying gay men and AIDS. His research approach aimed to uncover the ways in which individuals and groups participate in certain behaviours and communications, and the ways people collectively form their perceptions and respond to AIDS. In the description of four constructions of HIV, he differentiated the 'moralistic' framework, the 'contagion' framework model, the 'political' problem and the 'medical' construction. Polgar (1996) later building on his work, to summarise various understandings of AIDS in the historical contexts, in public attitudes and with moral considerations, proposed a typology of five different social constructions that underlie the professional and public understanding and explanation of HIV & AIDS. His five models—**medical, epidemic, organisational (economic), moral** and **political**, clearly distinguishes different power relationships, dominant metaphors and symbols, the most pressing questions and uncertainties discussed in different discourses. The research considers Polgar's (1996) 'Social constructions of HIV & AIDS: Theory and policy implications'. The model elucidates construction of sexual health in five categories (Polgar, 1996 as cited in Zhang, 2011):

1  In a **medical model**, science describes HIV scientifically and in the body, in terms of a compromised immune system, opportunistic infections, treatment and care.
2  An **epidemic model** identifies risk behaviours and transmission routes, informing health education and disease prevention. Organisational conceptions of AIDS developed by large interests, particularly hospitals, according to economic, administrative, and health concerns.
3  Social constructions of HIV & AIDS as plague or punishment against society are advanced by moralists who equate HIV with taboo social and sexual behaviour thus constructing the **Moralistic model**.
4  **Economic/ Political constructions** of AIDS highlight public health in the face of obstacles to treatment and the delivery of services to people living with HIV. Political and moral constructs are at odds over AIDS as a form of social stigma, magnifying many forms of prejudice and discrimination.

Each construct is supported by an institutional authority, framing the problems and responses to HIV & AIDS, the dominant metaphors and symbols, and the most pressing questions and uncertainties. Specially, the medical model examines AIDS as a disease from a scientific and biomedical perspective; the epidemic model explains AIDS in terms of its transmission and prevention within a socio-cultural context; the organisational (economic) model targets the issues and problems within health administrations and organisations; the moral model interprets AIDS from the religious beliefs and perceptions; and the political model focuses on the state's political agenda. Table 3.1 provides a detailed summary of the five models. These theoretical discussions have expanded from the biomedical paradigm to the social construction of HIV & AIDS drawing perspectives from sociology, anthropology and linguistics. This chapter reviewed literature relating to the social construction theory. An historical overview of the population control programmes in India and its relation to HIV & AIDS scenario places the study in the cultural context in which it was conducted. It also examined early literature and discussed the theoretical frameworks used in the development and the analysis of this study.

## The politics of HIV & AIDS: International policy frameworks

Citizens in developed countries with the best indicators of sexual health regard sexual expression as a normal part of growing up. It is usually viewed as a healthy biological, social, emotional and cultural process. In such countries sexual health is promoted by non-judgmental attitudes of adults and by mass media campaigns (Lottes, 2002). Sex education in school, easy availability of contraceptives and counselling are the mainstay in these countries while addressing the issues upon sexual health. National health insurance covers most of the cost of sexual health services that encourages young and old. Sexual health in developed countries is based on value of rights, responsibility and respect. The government and the general society consider it not only a duty to provide accurate information and confidential contraceptive services to the masses, but view such provision of services and information as their rights. In turn there is no attempt to motivate behaviour of masses through a collective effort to demand abstinence as seen in developing countries. Therefore, the goal is not to prevent the masses from having sex but to educate and empower them to make responsible decisions. The major expectation is that the majority will act responsibly to try to avoid pregnancy and STDs (Lottes, 2002). The public health policies in such countries are based on public health research and input from well-trained sex educators, not on political or religious definitions of sexual behaviour. In the process, most of the developed countries have come up with their own definitions of sexual health in reference to their citizens. Thereby, policies related to sexual health with reference to HIV & AIDS were formulated in these countries. The past few years ever since the advent of HIV & AIDS, has shown an increasing use

*Table 3.1* Polgar's five social constructions of HIV & AIDS

|  | Medical | Epidemic | Organisational | Moral | Political |
|---|---|---|---|---|---|
| **Institutional authority** | Science and bio-medicine | Behaviour science | Health administration | Religion | State |
| **Authority type** | Rational, scientific | Cultural | Bureaucratic | Religion | Political, economic |
| **Problems with HIV** | Virus infection, HIV-disease, AIDS | Risk behaviour, health services | Occupational health, organisational dynamics | Individual standards, behaviours | Unequal impact, silence and neglect |
| **Major response** | Research testing and treatment | Public education and prevention campaigns | Specialisa-tions, universal precautions | Abstain, avoid restrict contact | Protest, educate, resist, survive |
| **AIDS metaphors** | Virus, bodily disease | Epidemic, STD. Social disease | Infectious disease, Occupational hazard | Fall from grace, sin, evil | Danger, Health problem |
| **Symbols of HIV risk** | Blood, medical waste, uni-versal pre-cautions, color codes and barriers | Geo-graphic, graphic and numeric indicators, safer sex and injecting supplies | Organisational behaviour, infections, prescriptions | (Gay) plague | Stigma |
| **Major questions, uncertainties** | Best medi-cal Treat-ments HIV and immunity functions, vaccina-tion and cure | Infection and trans-mission routes and rates, prevention effective-ness | Safety requirement, allocations of resources, non-discrimination | Moral behaviour, protection of innocence | Responsi-bility, account-ability, accessibility |

(Adapted from Zhang, 2011).

of the concept of sexual health. This upsurge is especially noticeable not only in the field of health education and promotion but also in academic sources. The concept is typically used self-evidently and with widely diverse connotations. The definition and understanding of sexual health are still evolving and pose various critical questions. For instance, the term sexual health may imply various risks, including a one-sided health perspective on sexuality and a new excuse to control sexual behaviour. The recent discourse on sexual health is paralleled by an upsurge in the debate on sexual rights. Both concepts serve different functions but are intricately interwoven. The literature on construction of health and disease suggests that feeling healthy is best understood within social norms (Kovács, 1998). These social norms are specific to the society in which one lives. The biological adaptation to changes in body or health as a response to environment, and even health as a process of meeting expectations of the society in which one lives can be explained by the normative view of health (Nordenfelt, 1987). Sickness was a moral category and people were held responsible for their illness. The development of a scientific discourse has replaced this religious framework. Within the scientific discourse, illness is explained in natural terms, resulting from causal agents such as germs and viruses. Within this profane framework, individuals are no longer held morally responsible for an illness (Sandfort & Ehrhardt, 2004:182). It becomes pertinent to understand the processes of how the concept of sexual health awareness is being inculcated into the masses. The empirical research in health, sexuality and gender has demonstrated how understanding practices vary across different times and settings. Comparative studies of socio-cultural issues are rare, however and these too may contribute to the literature, to policy formulation and in particular, to understanding how it is appropriate to attempt to transfer models for HIV prevention from one socio-cultural context to another. This section examines the policy frameworks of different countries that are seeking to combat the epidemic—HIV & AIDS. Policies in each country are guided by the higher prevalence of HIV & AIDS in its target audience. Policies vary by country, political system and the prevailing customs and mores. But, eventually they are based mostly on actual experiences of the government in tackling the epidemic. The objective here is to analyse the approaches adopted on sexual health in Netherlands, Finland, Lesotho, Swaziland, Uganda and Thailand which could offer lessons for India. These countries have been chosen deliberately for this study. The Netherlands and Finland have been chosen as these countries fare much better in HIV prevalence rates and the containing the spread of the virus in the major part of the population (UNAIDS, 2012). The Netherlands' tourism (Anders et al., 1999; Wonders & Michalowski, 2001) and Thailand's (Leheny, 1995; Nuttavuthisit, 2007) have a dubious distinction of rampant prostitution as well as of promoting sex. Swaziland, Lesotho and Uganda have been chosen from the African continent where the prevalence rates are very high. Uganda is most of the time talked of as the success model for HIV prevention and this country is referred to as a model nation which most of the African nations should emulate (Green et al., 2006; Parkhurst, 2004). Cross-national comparisons not only serve as a means of gaining a better understanding of different societies, their structures, and institutions but have also contributed in the area of social policy as a means of evaluating the solutions adopted for dealing with similar kinds of problems (Hantrais, 1996). Thus, I have tried to examine the various policies, strategies adopted and the general response to the epidemic by each country. Comparisons pertaining to these countries were made through perusal of policy guidelines, articles, documents and the annual reports submitted by the countries to UNAIDS that are available on the internet. The analysis of the counties was taken based on a framework such as status of the epidemic at the time of writing this chapter, National response to the epidemic, which included brief policy and programmatic responses of that country and the prominent communication approaches adopted for prevention. The primary objective here is to analyse the sexual health policies of six different countries. A study of such policies could offer lessons for policy formulation in India based on their long-term experiences in dealing and communicating about sexual health. They were analysed on the parameters on how sexual health is regarded in that country, how the policy guidelines were formulated and on what basis. The documents also helped in understanding what role the media played in the disseminating messages on sexual health.

### Netherlands

#### Status of the epidemic

The Netherlands has a concentrated HIV epidemic, that is particularly higher in the specific sub population such as Men having Sex with Men (MSM) and migrants (UNAIDS and WHO, 2000 as cited in UNGASS, 2012b). The Dutch government attributes this to the high level of migration from high prevalence countries. The basic notion in Netherlands is that HIV & AIDS is primarily fuelled by transmission among MSM. The National Institute for Public Health and the Environment (RIVM) in its 2009 report states:

> The number of HIV-infected individuals (15–70 years) living in the Netherlands on 1 January 2008 has been estimated to be 21,500 (19,000–24,000). This represents an increase of about 10% in comparison with the previous estimate in 15–49-year-olds from 2005. The estimated HIV infection prevalence remained at 0.2% in the adult population. Of the HIV infections in January 2008, 55% were estimated to be attributed to MSM transmission, 40% to heterosexual contacts and 4% to intravenous drug use (IDU).[1]

The UNGASS country report (2012b) on Netherlands outlines that on 1 June 2011, the largest group was MSM (58%). Heterosexuals accounted for 31% of patients (16% of men and 86% of women). Heterosexuals included a considerable proportion of individuals originating from other countries than the Netherlands (32% originated from the Netherlands).

#### National response to the epidemic

The Dutch government sought to place HIV & AIDS policy in a larger framework of sexual health. The Dutch government formulated the National

Policy Plan on STI/HIV 2012–16. Its primary objective was to 'to renew and reinforce' the Dutch HIV/STI policy (UNGASS, 2012b:5). The national note on health policy-2011 addresses the multiple health issues, lifestyle policy and issues related to sexual health. The division of responsibilities was mainly organised by risk groups and served to promote tailor-made approaches based on appropriate expertise. The groups identified in the STI/HIV prevention plan were:

- MSM;
- Migrants (primarily those from HIV-endemic countries);
- Young people;
- Sex workers and their clients;
- Drug users;
- HIV-infected persons.

Human rights aspects such as universal access to comprehensive prevention programme, treatment, care and support constitute a fundamental principle in the Netherlands. The promotion of safe (sexual) practices by provision of information is an important component of primary HIV & AIDS prevention. In this regard schools play an important role in informing youth although comprehensive sexuality education is not obligatory in Netherlands. The promotion of safe (sexual) practices by provision of information is an important component of primary HIV & AIDS prevention. In this regard schools play an important role in informing youth and comprehensive sexuality education, which has been made obligatory from 2012 onwards. Youth healthcare services also provide information about safe sex practices.

*Prominent communication approaches*

Information about safe sex and prevention of STI/HIV is communicated by means of national information campaigns in Netherlands.

> Information about safe sex and prevention of STI/HIV is mainly communicated by means of targeted communication activities for specific groups such as MSM, migrants, sex workers, IDU, and youth. In general, NGOs play key roles in primary prevention of HIV by provision of information, especially among high risk groups. Information activities utilize internet, printed materials, peer-to-peer education, outreach activities.
>
> (UNGASS, 2012b:13)

A main communication initiative is the national *vrij veilig* (I play safe, or I don't play at all) campaign by STI/HIV—Netherlands in 2011. The purpose of this campaign was to encourage young people to use condoms before they have sex. The campaign ran from 1 December to 31 December 2011. The

Dutch government also has a specific regulation ('Aanvullende Curatieve Soa-bestrijding' [ACS]) that provides low-threshold and free-of-charge STI/HIV testing and care for high-risk groups. In 2008, the ACS regulation was supplemented with an additional regulation that caters to young people under the age of 25 years ('Aanvullende Seksualiteitshulpverlening' [ASH]). The ASH regulation offers low-threshold services that can support youth with questions and problems regarding sexuality. Consultation services are offered with the support of governmental funds of about €3.5 million per year. In addition, a related website and a toolkit on sexual health was also developed. The Netherlands deserves attention, for it being the Western country that has had the lowest rates of unplanned pregnancy, abortion and teen pregnancy for quite some time. The pragmatic and ethical approaches adopted by the Dutch for sexual health programmes allow an open discussion about sexual issues and encourage adolescents to talk about sex and topics that interest them. The attitude of the government is that both the public and families have a responsibility to help and people avoid unwanted pregnancies and STDs. The goal of such initiative is to instil a sense of responsibility in the young and to give them the knowledge to act accordingly. It is also important the general public is tolerant and accepting of teenage sexual experiences. The view is that it is impossible and quite ridiculous to try to prevent teenagers from having sex. Thus, a sensible action is to prepare them to act responsibly and not enforce abstinence upon them. A major component in the Dutch approach to sexual health is their mass media campaign.

According to Berne & Huberman (1999:13–14)

> These campaigns help to keep sexual health on the public agenda, reduce stigma by emphasizing community responsibility for health problems, serve in educating youth by providing a catalyst for discussion and reinforcing messages, reach higher risk groups not generally accessible through traditional channels, encourage intermediaries (teachers, youth workers, pharmacists) to draw attention to safer sex, and stimulate organizations to provide training and education to intermediaries.

One of the media campaigns in the Netherlands popularised the use of the slogan 'Double Dutch'—meaning to use the double protection of a condom (to lower STD risk) and the pill (for protection against pregnancy) when having sex. Media campaigns are well coordinated with the education and health sectors to ensure consistency and accuracy of messages to the young. Additional strategies used by clinics that provide sexual health services to Dutch include (a) accept teen sexuality and sexual behaviour, (b) guarantee anonymity or confidentiality, (c) waive pap smears and pelvic exams as prerequisites for initial contraceptives, (d) provide non-judgmental service and (e) require minimal paperwork and no parental consent. With several port cities, STDs are also a major public health concern in the Netherlands. In order to keep health risks minimal in Netherlands, accessible and government-funded

STD clinics provide testing, treatment, education, pre- and post-health insurance (which covers over 99% of the Dutch population) funds all reproductive health services except condoms. These include contraceptive pills and devices for emergency contraception, abortion, testing for pregnancy and HIV/STD, prenatal care, delivery and all drug therapy associated with diagnosis and treatment of STD, HIV & AIDS. Stigmatisation and incidents of discrimination due to HIV infection is still a problem in Dutch society. The government has sustained its policy to increase knowledge about STI/HIV and thereby, among other things, seeks to reduce stigmatisation and discrimination due to HIV & AIDS. The Ministry of VWS maintains the position that HIV-infected individuals should not be prosecuted for unsafe sex unless coercion, deception, or disparities in terms of power are involved. This is consistent with the notion that everyone carries a responsibility for his or her own health. Since August 2009, legislation (*Arbeidsomstandighedenwet*) against discrimination on the work place has been strengthened. Employers are obliged to have developed a policy based on risk assessment and evaluation to prevent and handle incidents of discrimination. Discrimination based on medical conditions or handicap (thus including HIV & AIDS) is prohibited. This applies to discrimination between employees and employers as well as among employees. The Labour Inspectorate (*Arbeidsinspectie*) supervises the implementation of this legislation. General social acceptance of risk groups, such as MSM, can contribute to the success of initiatives throughout the full spectrum of the HIV & AIDS prevention and response efforts. A policy document, compiled by a coordinating ministry and with the contributions of several stakeholders, outlines the policy to enhance social acceptance of MSM (UNGASS, 2012b).

### Finland

#### Status of the epidemic

Finland is one of the five Nordic states. Nordic countries are distinguished by their comprehensive welfare states, which are based on egalitarian notions of the community and individual social rights. HIV & AIDS in Finland from the start was backed by a strong managerial response by various societal institutions. It arrived in Finland as a 'killer' disease in 1983 amidst frenzied tabloid stories and reporters lurking around AIDS clinics to photograph patients (Clarke, 2002). Through the years, AIDS in Finland has predominately been associated in public discourse with gays, foreigners, foreign prostitutes and drug users, those excluded from 'normal' societies who seldom have public faces, lives, or voices.

> HIV/AIDS has thus progressed from a subject of deep anxiety in the 1980s, when metaphors drawn from horror movies were the norm, to a blasé boredom coupled with denial amidst an increasing sense that HIV

& AIDS only affects deviants and no longer constitutes a threat to the Finnish nation.

(Clarke, 2002:21)

Despite Finland's early adoption of WHO guidelines on voluntary testing, access to treatment and patient rights, fears of discrimination and social exclusion remained strong amongst people living with HIV & AIDS.

At the end of year 2011 the cumulative total of diagnosed HIV positive individuals in Finland was 2953 (2133 males and 820 females). Cumulatively 580 AIDS cases—including 299 AIDS deaths—had been reported. The most affected groups are men having sex with men, migrants from high prevalence areas and people who inject drugs. In 2010 and 2011, 187 and 177 new cases of HIV-infection, respectively, were reported; most of them were associated with sexual transmission. The number of AIDS deaths was 5 in 2011 and 8 in 2010.

(UNGASS, 2012:3)

Finland again provides another fine example of a country whose changes in sexual health policy resulted in better indicators of sexual health for its population. In the 1970s a new abortion law made abortion legal and education on how to provide such a service was provided at hospitals. When the abortion law was passed, the goal was to make abortion an uncommon event, and so every effort was made to provide comprehensive contraceptive information and services. The government mandated that family planning and maternity/infant/child health services be provided free or at low cost in all local health centres. Rimpela (1998), one of Finland's sexual health experts, attributes the good sexual health outcomes to five factors: the use of preventive approaches to public health; a change of focus from abortion to the prevention of its main cause, unintended pregnancy; excellent cooperation and coordination between the health and education sectors; strong and skilled guidance from the national health authorities; and professional attitudes and skills of nurses and doctors in sex education and family planning. Moreover, Finns do not take a moralistic approach to sexuality and the sexual activity of the young. The emphasis is on helping teenagers make responsible sexual decisions by providing them with adequate knowledge and skills (Lottes, 2002).

## National response to the epidemic

A main objective of the Finnish HIV & AIDS prevention policy is prevention of new infections, which is the key target of policy measures. For those who become infected, there is guaranteed free access to medically indicated treatment and care. Support for full social empowerment of persons who have been infected to reduce their vulnerability is an essential part of prevention policies. Prevention activities are managed through national coordination and a multidisciplinary public/private partnership approach. The overall aim of the strategy is to control the HIV prevalence among the Finnish population.

The essential elements for the success of the national strategy (UNGASS, 2012:8) are:

1   Decreasing the risks for infection.
2   Effective use of commodities used in prevention of transmission such as male and female condoms, sterile injecting equipment, medicines.
3   Reducing the harms and impacts of HIV infection; ensuring the integration of people living with HIV into the mainstream of society, ensuring the best available prevention, treatment, care and support, and prevention of discrimination.

The Ministry of Social Affairs and Health (2007) in Finland compiled the first national action programme for the promotion of sexual and reproductive health. Sexual health counselling is integrated into basic services as well as preventive and medical treatment. The programme points out the importance of screening and counselling the young, particularly during the first visit of counselling, concerning prevention of pregnancy. HIV testing is provided free of charge in all municipal health care centres and it is available also in private health care services. The screening of chlamydia trachomatis (all under 25 years of age) and the human papilloma virus vaccination is expected to work together with the sexual education to decrease the amount of sexually transmitted diseases. HIV & AIDS prevention is integrated into school health and sexual health education. Finland has supported nationally the development of the HIV vaccine by providing both investment and project support.

*Prominent communication approaches*

Starting from its initial silence on the issue, the communication campaign can be summed up thus:

> HIV & AIDS remains a deeply stigmatized disease in Finland. Information campaigns by the Finnish Red Cross have tended to promote safe sex by fear (as illness) rather than through health promotion.
>
> (Clarke, 2002:24)

HIV testing practices and anti-discriminatory legislation such as the reform of the Communicable Diseases Act and patients' rights laws became the focus of the Finnish AIDS Council. Its main objective was to protect the rights of Finns living with HIV & AIDS. Clarke (2002) also states that most of the HIV & AIDS campaigns in Finland portrayed it as an external threat—a souvenir brought home by its citizens from visits abroad.

A recent campaign had large posters at bus stops with a simple arrow pointing outwards with a text stating 'He might have HIV too'. When watching people at the bus stop near my home, I noticed that people inevitably moved away from the arrow to stand elsewhere.

(Clarke, 2002:27)

HIV & AIDS and foreigners assumed a dangerous combination in Finland. It also did not have any community-based infrastructure to deal with the issues of migrants. It also had difficulties dealing with human rights, racial discrimination and difficulties associated with living in Finland. As a result of which, migrants continued to remain on the fringes of the Finnish society. The Finnish government started the campaign 'travel safety' in 2008 in order to reduce HIV and STI transmission and to promote diagnosis among travellers.

Safe sex advice, condoms and lubricants were delivered at the ports, airports and border crossings to Russia twice a year. The aim of the campaign is also to train health professionals in HIV and safe sex counselling for travelers.

(UNGASS, 2012:10)

The Finnish Broadcasting company, YLE radio channel, organises an annual summer campaign 'Kesäkumi (summer rubber)' every year. Its main aim is to prevent spread of STIs among youth. The campaign talks openly about STIs, often with young celebrities, who participate in the campaign by performing in radio spots. During the campaign free condoms are delivered to summer festivals and concerts. At the same time, the new recruits who start their military service during the summer also get information on STIs and free condoms through this radio channel.

## *Uganda*

### *Status of the epidemic*

In Uganda, the epidemic is still predominantly heterosexually transmitted with 80% of infections. The Mode of Transmission Study (2008) study indicated that the risk factors responsible for the spread of HIV transmission are of two types, namely, modifiable and non-modifiable. The modifiable risk factors comprise of multiple partnerships, HIV sero-discordance (Where one person is HIV positive and the other is negative), inconsistent condom use, infection with sexually transmitted infections (STIs) especially Herpes Simplex Virus (HSV)-2 and lack of male circumcision while the non-modifiable factors include urban residence, older age, being married or formerly married, being female and residence in northern Uganda, implying the need for focused interventions among these groups. The Uganda AIDS Indicator

Survey (UAIS, 2011) indicated that comprehensive knowledge of HIV & AIDS is at 33.8% for women in age group 15–49 and 41.1% for men in the same group. Women who know that HIV can be transmitted by breastfeeding and risk of mother-to-child transmission (MTCT) can be reduced by mothers taking special drugs during pregnancy is 65.2% while only 55.7% of the men are in the know. Circumcision stands only at 23.6% among men in age group 15–49. The National HIV Prevention Strategy 2010 documented that an estimated 1.2 million people in Uganda are HIV infected, of whom 57% are females and 13% children aged less than 15 years. On the other hand, cases of new infection were estimated at 124,000 (Global AIDS Response Progress Report, Uganda AIDS Commission, 2012 as cited in UNGASS, 2012e). In Uganda, the national average adult HIV prevalence reduced from a high of 18.5 % in 1992 to about 5% in 2000 due to, among other reasons, strong political leadership, an open approach to combating the epidemic and a strong multi-sectoral, decentralised and community response (UNGASS, 2012e:1)

During the beginning of the African epidemic, Uganda faced a severe crisis, with almost 30% of the adult population infected with HIV & AIDS in 1980s and 1990s. 'Uganda responded through a mix of rationalist and creative policy approaches and after a decade of intervention a decline in HIV prevalence was observed' (Mohammed, 2003:262) Since 2000, the global AIDS debate has been dominated by two major issues, namely the rising prevalence levels in Southern Africa, China, India and the Russian Federation on the one hand, and the claims of the Ugandan miracle, its possible causes and lessons on the other. As De Waal (2003) as cited in Tumushabe, (2006) points out, the Ugandan HIV & AIDS 'success story' has been so politically important for the government and the international HIV & AIDS 'industry' that it has rarely been subjected to careful scrutiny. Uganda was experiencing a full blown-epidemic by the late 1980s; the virulence of which was exacerbated by social dislocation and insecurity related to economic crisis and war (Putzel, 2004). In 1998, an estimated 1.9 million people were living with HIV & AIDS in Uganda (UNAIDS, 1999). AIDS had overtaken malaria as a leading cause of death among people aged 12–49 years and was responsible for 12% of all deaths. As the epidemic continued to spread and intensify in Africa and other areas of the world in the early and mid-1990s, prevalence rates in Uganda were reported to be declining, especially starting around 1993. International and bilateral aid agencies that provide large sums of money for HIV prevention used Uganda as an example to argue that, with sufficient resources and appropriate prevention messages, HIV & AIDS could be controlled. HIV & AIDS programme in Uganda, like elsewhere, had a bumpy start. With donor support, the AIDS Control Programme (ACP) started a mass education campaign about HIV & AIDS using scare messages on radio and television that promoted abstinence and condom use. Little did the programme implementers know that such messages were increasing stigma and discrimination against People Living with HIV & AIDS

(PLWHA), and hence driving the epidemic underground. Until 1990, there was no condom distribution system and the influential church groups strongly criticised their use. With the end of the cold war, Western donors set the democratization of politics, good governance and prudent management of the economy as standards for continued donor assistance to Africa (Tumushabe, 2006:9).

## National response to the epidemic

HIV & AIDS prevention efforts were re-launched in 2010 and 2011. The Uganda AIDS Commission (UAC) Board was re-constituted at this time. The National HIV and AIDS Policy was developed and disseminated between 2010 and 2011. The National Strategic Plan was reviewed and on World AIDS Day 2011, the revised NSP was re-launched. This approach was expected to re-invigorate the fight against the epidemic.

The goals of the revised NSP were to (UNGASS, 2012e:2):

a   reduce HIV incidence by 30% by 2015;
b   improve the quality of life of People Living with HIV (PLHIV) by mitigating the health effects of HIV & AIDS by 2015;
c   improve the level of access of services for PLHIV, Orphans and Vulnerable Children and other vulnerable populations by 2015; and
d   build an effective and efficient system that ensures quality, equitable and timely service delivery by 2015.

The national prevention strategic plan and eight sector prevention strategic plans were developed and launched during this time. In general, during the period 2010 and 2011, many policy documents and guidelines were developed and disseminated. These policies, plans and guidelines increased the momentum already achieved in the national response. The revised plan also improved on the country's chance of realising its vision of a population free of HIV and its effect.

## Prominent communication approaches

Ugandans seemed to communicate about AIDS and people with AIDS differently (Tumushabe 2006). However, in Uganda personal channels of communication amongst the population predominated in communicating about AIDS in both urban and rural areas, among men and women. Personal networks became the dominant channels that could be stratified by urban (74%) and rural areas (84%), and among men (70%) (Low-Beer & Stoneburner, 2003). There was a shift from mainstream media to personal channels for communicating about AIDS between 1989 and 1995 (Green et al., 2006). A second distinctive component in Uganda was knowledge through social networks of someone with or who had died of AIDS (Low-Beer & Stoneburner,

2003). This indicates that AIDS issues in Uganda were rooted in discussions in social networks rather than just received from public health and media messages. Ugandans in a way communicated about AIDS and people with AIDS, reflected and influenced their behavioural response. The horizontal behavioural and communication process was widely mobilised by faith-based organisations, prominent cultural figures, political, military and community figures, NGOs and care organisations like TASO (The AIDS Support Organisation).

There were also distinctive vertical policies in Uganda that helped scale this horizontal, community response (Low-Beer & Stoneburner, 2003:6):

1   a clear, direct communication programme focused on three clear topics: AIDS, reducing sexual partners or 'zero grazing' and not pointing fingers but caring for people with AIDS.
2   AIDS case surveillance which gave a definitive diagnosis and form to the AIDS epidemic at local level and allowed all involved, health personnel, families and communities to talk and deal with AIDS directly.
3   Legitimation and strong primary support of care networks with a broad approach involving NGOs like TASO and faith-based organizations (which talked about AIDS in community events including funerals).

This focus on communication, behaviour change and care is only the basis of HIV prevention. It needs to be added along with condom provision, HIV and STD treatment and when feasible the development of vaccines. However, despite more sophisticated approaches elsewhere, the basic communication and behavioural process that were identified in Uganda may be necessary for HIV prevention to be successfully scaled to an international level.

### Lesotho

#### Status of the epidemic

Lesotho has the third highest HIV prevalence in the world. However, in 2011 it signalled towards a decreasing trend (UNGASS, 2012a:11):

> In 2011, Lesotho's HIV prevalence rate for adults (15 to 49 years) remained at 23% signaling a continuing stabilization of the epidemic. However, gender disparities in HIV prevalence remain: 26.7% of all adult women are HIV-positive as compared to 18% of all adult men. Approximately 60% of all HIV-positive adults and children are female.

Lesotho took a substantial amount of time in responding after the first AIDS case was reported due to poor finances and infrastructure. The HIV epidemic continues to be fuelled by inter-relationships between both behavioural and structural drivers such as multiple and concurrent sexual partnerships; inadequate levels of HIV-testing and personal knowledge of HIV status; inadequate frequency of condom use across all sexually active population group; slow progress for adolescents and youth to change patterns of sexual behaviour; high rates of alcohol use; and low demand for voluntary, health-facility-based male circumcision. These factors were compounded by the structural factors such as social and cultural factors (UNGASS, 2012a). The Government of Lesotho announced the multi-sectoral National AIDS Strategic Plan, which intended to reduce HIV prevalence by 5%, increase annual condom use by 50% and provide care for half of Lesotho's AIDS orphans, all by 2003[2]. In 2001, the Lesotho AIDS Programme Coordinating Authority (LAPCA) that aimed to mobilise resources to coordinate the national AIDS response, improve information and communication on HIV & AIDS and improve sentinel surveillance of HIV constrained LAPCA's capacity. King Letsie III declared HIV & AIDS a national disaster in 2003.

### National response to the epidemic

The 'Know Your Status' campaign with the support of the World Health Organisation, the Global Fund and the United Nations Development Programme was undertaken by the Government of Lesotho in 2004. This campaign intended to overcome the stigma and discrimination that surrounds testing publicly for HIV & AIDS. Under this scheme, trained community health workers approached every single household with rapid HIV tests. Everyone tested and counselled would then be referred to post-test services according to their HIV status. The Government of Lesotho's Know Your Status (KYS) Campaign Plan 2006–7 relied on communities to choose how testing and counselling should be progressively rolled out. Structural conditions such as poverty and rural isolation hindered the roll out of the local services. Lesotho's lack of health care workers proved a further obstacle to the testing campaign. The Government of Lesotho has implemented several HIV prevention strategies, including educational campaigns, work-based HIV prevention initiatives, the targeting of high-risk groups and prevention of mother-to-child transmission. The new National HIV and AIDS Strategic Plan (NSP) was launched on 1 December 2011. The NSP incorporates Lesotho's universal access commitments under the 2011 Political Declaration on HIV & AIDS as well as its Millennium Development Goals. The priorities listed out in the plan were (UNGASS, 2012a:12):

- To accelerate and intensify HIV prevention in order to reduce new annual HIV infections by 50%;
- To scale up universal access to comprehensive and quality-assured care, treatment and support;
- To strengthen coping mechanisms for vulnerable individuals, groups and households; and,

- To improve the efficiency and effectiveness of coordination of the national multisectoral HIV and AIDS response.

The National BCC Strategy was formulated in 2010. It disseminated multimedia materials targeting various stakeholders such as adolescents and youth that addressed multiple and concurrent partnerships. It also attempted to promote more male involvement in HIV prevention.

*Prominent communication approaches*

An interactive educational 'road show' designed at increasing HIV awareness through talent shows, poetry, sports and dance, as well as life skills activities and educational tools was undertaken amongst the youth in 2005. HIV & AIDS as a topic was also included in both primary and secondary school curriculum in subjects such as health and physical education, science, agriculture, home economics and geography. Unfortunately, increasing numbers of young people are reportedly having sex before 15 years of age, with a rise in the number of young men having multiple partners. But the plans have been set back by financial constraints, severe shortages of health workers and the logistical difficulty of reaching parts of the population in mountainous and isolated rural areas in Lesotho. Communication campaigns in Lesotho regularly carry messages on male circumcision (UNGASS, 2012a); addresses stigma and discrimination, Diagnosis and treatment of sexually transmitted infections (STIs) and other services.

## Swaziland

*Status of the epidemic*

The number of people living with HIV in Swaziland in 2011 was estimated to be 173,619 adults and 21,780 children (UNGASS, 2012c). The Swaziland National AIDS Programme (SNAP) during its short-term plan (1986 to 1988), and later a medium-term plan (1989 to 1992) aimed at providing information and education on HIV; promote condom usage; manage the spread of sexually transmitted infections; and screen all donated blood. The HIV Modes of Transmission Study (2009) established that heterosexual contact among persons with one sexual partner is the main mode of HIV transmission in Swaziland. It indicated that, 62% of new infections occur among women and that almost two thirds (65%) of 100 new infections in Swaziland occur among those aged 25 years and older, many of whom one would expect to be married or cohabiting with a steady partner.

The Policy Document on HIV & AIDS and STD Prevention and Control (1998) intended to make education and communication 'the major weapon' against HIV and AIDS. The plans also aimed to improve care for those living with HIV; increase women's access to prevention services; scale up testing services; and further prevent the spread of STDs. The Crisis Management and Technical Committee (CMTC) developed the National Strategic Plan (2000–5) that focused on improving health services; changing behaviour through mass media outlets, schools and workplaces; and minimising the future impact of the epidemic, especially for vulnerable groups such as orphans. In 2001, CMTC was replaced by the NERCHA, or the National Emergency Response Council on HIV and AIDS, which evolved the National Strategic Framework for HIV and AIDS (2009–14) which came to be known as the 'three ones principle'—the One strategy and One Monitoring and Evaluation system (UNGASS, 2012c:3).

> The NSF introduced a paradigm shift in the planning landscape for HIV in the country by ushering a results and evidence based planning approach. An elaborate results framework has been developed that has concrete, evidence informed and time bound results at impact, outcome and output levels. The overall purpose of the NSF is to bring together stakeholders to work together towards achieving the common results.

Swaziland has also the distinction of introducing Geographic Information System (GIS)-based HIV reporting system in 2010, which would eventually improve the performance of national response to the epidemic. The use of maps in depicting service delivery became a useful tool to disseminate user friendly information which allowed immediate decision making thus linking monitoring to planning.

### National response to the epidemic

Swaziland introduced a number of laws, policies and programmes since the outbreak of the epidemic such as the People Trafficking and People Smuggling (Prohibition) Act 2009; the Employment Act of 1980 (as amended); Sexual Offences and Domestic Violence Bill (2010); National HIV Prevention Policy (2011); Stigma and Discrimination Index (2011); etc., to name a few (UNGASS, 2012c: 5–6). Swaziland in 2011 launched an initiative to circumcise between 125,000 and 175,000 HIV-negative males from 15 to 49 years of age in a 12-month period aiming to prevent HIV incidence in Swaziland by 75% by 2025, which failed eventually[3]. As elsewhere in sub-Saharan Africa, the huge number of people dying from AIDS in Swaziland exacerbates existing poverty, which in turn leaves individuals vulnerable to the adverse effects of HIV. When those of productive age die from AIDS or are too sick to work, there is less income and therefore less food for families. Lack of adequate food and nutrition leaves individuals less able to cope with HIV if they are infected, as effective treatment depends on a good diet. The deaths of many adults have left behind a youthful population in Swaziland. Around 39% of the population is under 14, and those over 65 only account for 3.7%. Many children are orphaned and left in the care of grandparents; and if they do not have any, they may be left to fend for themselves. Increasing economic decline pushed Swazis into further poverty or economic migration, potentially escalating the scale of the epidemic. The huge scale of AIDS-related illness and deaths is weakening the government's capacity to deliver health care and other services, with serious consequences for food security, economic growth and human development.

*Prominent communication approaches*

The Swaziland Demographic and Health Survey (2007) as cited in the UNGASS Country Report (2012c:14) states:

> Early sexual initiations coupled with inter-generational sex and late marriage present a risk of contracting HIV. The median age of sexual debut is 16 and 17 for women and men, respectively and 48% of women and 34% of men aged 18–24 begun their sexual relations by the age of 18. The median age of marriage is 26 years for women and 29 years for men aged 30–34.

In 2001, King Mswati III reinstated a custom that banned all girls under 18 from sexual activity for five years and required any man who has sex with a virgin to pay a cow to the girl's family. The policy, which required all girls to wear tassels to display their virginity, was widely criticised for demeaning girls and blaming women for the spread of HIV. Interestingly, the king was accused of ignoring his own policy when, in 2001, he became engaged to a 17-year-old girl. In 2005, the king called an end to the policy. Generally, King Mswati has been praised for speaking out about HIV & AIDS, however community organisations have said his sexual practices set a poor example. The king has numerous wives in accordance with the Swazi tradition of polygamy. In 2005, a campaign targeting young people was launched through billboard adverts, radio and the printed press, with slogans such as, 'Because tomorrow is mine', and, 'I want to finish my education. Sex can wait'. The UN has reported that almost two in three female Swazi secondary school students are following this advice and abstaining from sex until their late teens, however when they do become sexually active they face huge risks of acquiring HIV. In an attempt to combat the common Swazi practice of multiple partners, NERCHA launched a public HIV awareness campaign in 2006 under the siSwati title, *Makhwapheni Uyabulala*, or, 'Your secret lover will kill you'. Makhwapheni refers specifically to the 'secret lovers' of women. This focus met widespread criticism for its moralistic message that blamed women for the HIV epidemic and portrayed them as sexually irresponsible. The International Community of Women Living with HIV & AIDS claimed that the campaign 'failed to meaningfully involve people living with HIV & AIDS' (Avert, 2011 as cited in Chiwara 2012:22).

## *Thailand*

### Status of the epidemic

The first HIV & AIDS case was reported in 1984 in Thailand. Unsafe sex has been ascribed as the driving force for the spread of the epidemic amongst women and men of reproductive age. Key affected populations are: Female Sex Workers (FSW), Men Having Sex with Men (MSM) and People Who Inject Drugs (PWID) (UNGASS, 2012d).

Despite the stable and slightly declining trend of HIV prevalence among pregnant women aged 15–24 years and male military recruits aged 20–24 years, the risk behaviour data in youth which reported an increase in sex-partner mixing without condom use could be contributing to the increased risk for STIs and unwanted pregnancy. The age distribution of STI patients in which the highest number of cases was in the 15–24-year age group, and the number of teenage deliveries per 1,000 girls aged 15–19 years had increased from 33.7 in 1989 to 50.1 in 2010 (UNGASS, 2012d:2).

In any event, the spread of HIV in some provinces of Thailand is still severe, especially those which receive a large number of tourists, and provinces bordering on the eastern seaboard and Gulf of Thailand. HIV among MSM is higher in large urban centres and important tourist locations. In general, HIV infection among the population of international labour migrants is higher for those working in the fisheries industry than other occupations. This differential is possibly because of the nature of the work and higher sex risk behaviour of fishing boat crews. Sex workers in Thailand who are foreign migrants have higher levels of HIV than their Thai counterparts. Limitations of education and Thai illiteracy are barriers to accessing information and services for prevention of HIV and STIs. In sum, the epidemiological and behavioural data indicate that the number of new HIV infections in Thailand has not decreased. A trend of increasing spread of HIV is noted in the population of adolescents, and HIV prevalence remains high in the traditionally higher-risk populations and shows no indications of declining any time soon.

### National response to the epidemic

The UNDP (2004:22) in its report—*Thailand's Response to HIV & AIDS: Progress and Challenges* states:

> Thailand has shown that a well-funded, politically-supported and shrewdly-implemented response can change the course of the HIV & AIDS epidemic. After peaking at 143,000 in 1991, the annual number of new HIV infections has fallen to about 19,000 in 2003—making Thailand one of a handful of countries to have reversed a serious HIV & AIDS epidemic.

HIV & AIDS has had an adverse impact on Thailand's health systems, and socio-economic status of the country. Thailand has been undertaking measures to achieve consistent HIV & AIDS coverage through public media campaigns, condom promotion, prevention in youth and most-at-risk population groups. The HIV & AIDS prevention programmes are carried out in a three-pronged manner: (1) public information campaigns; (2) strengthening the HIV prevention networks; and (3) finding ways to ensure sustainability at the provincial and local administrative organisation levels to accelerate and take ownership of the HIV & AIDS prevention agenda. As target populations are identified in the National AIDS Plan, the HIV prevention programmes in Thailand are mostly targeting specific population groups. Most-at-risk population groups are very important and have received greater attention. This can be seen from policy and plan to reduce new infections by half by 2011 in IDU, MSM, female sex workers, prisoners and migrants in Thailand. The national programme is working intensively with all these groups using both domestic and international funding (GFATM). It is well recognised that to increase access to HIV prevention among these population groups needs outreach services by civil society organisations and linkage with services of hospitals, for which health service providers have to understand sex/gender/ sexuality issue in order to make their services friendly to the target populations. Most of this portion of the national programme is supported by the Global Fund to Fight AIDS, Tuberculosis and Malaria (GFATM). Nevertheless, the strategy for youth behaviour change has not had optimal effect since Thai youth are increasingly diverse in terms of attitudes, beliefs and lifestyles. It is still an important challenge for the programme to tailor strategies for youth to the various different lifestyles that are currently in fashion. Promotion of comprehensive sexuality education is still a weak point of the programme. The challenge here is to find a way to institutionalise comprehensive sexuality education in the school system through policy improvements at the national and ministerial level. There is no core curriculum at the national level that is acceptable to the Ministry of Education (MoE). The attitude of the MoE administrators and teachers still is not accepting of the need for comprehensive sexuality education. In any case, comprehensive sexuality education alone probably is insufficient to change attitudes and behaviours over the long-term since youth have different ways of learning as they mature into adolescence and adulthood. In addition, there are many variables to consider such as increased ease of access to sinful (risky) temptations and peer pressure (Sthapitanonda et al., 2003 cited in Malikhao, 2005).

*Prominent communication approaches*

When HIV & AIDS emerged in Thailand, the government thought that tourism would get affected and cause public panic (Malikhao, 2005). The Ministry of Public Health played a pivotal role in the National AIDS campaign, '100% condom use in brothels', which was the most prominent campaign carried out between 1989 and 1992. The objective of the campaign was to prevent sex clients from purchasing sexual services unless they used a condom. The National AIDS Foundation of Thailand was set up in 1997.

A summary of 26 research projects on mass media and HIV & AIDS in Thailand, executed during 1990–96 states:

> Negative messages frightening the public were the most prominent communication strategy applied in the initial period, mainly transmitted through government ads on television. The messages brand the people who contracted HIV negatively. The public's reaction was to negate or ignore news about HIV & AIDS, and to discriminate against infected people. This created misunderstanding among the public and caused anxiety and hopelessness among infected people.
>
> (Malikhao, 2005:308)

Thereafter, the social marketing approach gradually shifted to the use of positive campaign strategies. Top-down approaches, such as those giving moral support, avoiding branding names or creating emotional appeal, are widely used now by the Ministry of Public Health and other governmental organisations. (Sthapitanonda et al., 2003 as cited in Malikhao, 2005). However, from 1997 onwards another shift became visible, which got referred to as the bottom-up approach. The practice of using religion to help fight HIV & AIDS was adopted by Thailand.

## Comparative analysis

This section offers an analysis of the main aspects of HIV & AIDS and the strategies adopted by each country. The aim here is to draw on the provisions that could inform the suggestions for India on how to tackle the epidemic. All the countries examined are affected by HIV & AIDS in one way or the other. The only thing that differentiates them from each other is the population which is highly affected. Thereby, the policies, approaches and communication strategies are formulated to cater to them. The Netherlands and Finland are primarily worried about HIV transmission amongst the MSM and IDUs. The governments in these countries feel that it is the youth who fall in this category and have to be addressed adequately. The developed countries are at an advantage than the developing countries because of free condom provision and free national health insurance that covers most aspects of sexual health of the youth and the infected. Their (developed countries) main concerns are the migrants and travellers who they feel would bring in the virus, when migrating from affected countries for livelihood. Developed countries are also equally concerned with their own citizens getting HIV infected due to their promiscuous behaviour while visiting the affected countries. In such a situation, HIV & AIDS gets another mode of entry. Communication and prevention strategies are basically on monitoring the foreign trips made by its citizens and promoting condom usage by them. Both Netherlands and Finland have also focused on aspects of sexuality in youth by accepting the fact of teenage sexual encounters and addressing teenage pregnancies without any moral judgments. Abstinence is not demanded from the teenagers as witnessed in countries like Uganda, Lesotho, Swaziland and Thailand. The countries discussed previously have predominantly used religion and religious leaders as one of the channels to communicate with the masses about HIV & AIDS. Particularly, Uganda, which is often quoted as a 'success story' for HIV & AIDS worldwide, has used Faith-Based Organisations (FBOs) to the optimum. Similarly, Netherlands and Finland have used cultural leaders or rock stars to disseminate the HIV & AIDS messages among the masses. It can also be inferred here that Lesotho as well as Swaziland have used the churches as well as FBOs for tackling the HIV & AIDS menace. Uganda, Lesotho and Swaziland have been toying with the idea of circumcision, but with limited impacts amongst its population. At the same time, UNDP's report on Thailand (2004) warns that the HIV epidemic is getting worse. It states that the demand and supply for commercial/casual sex has increased manifold. This is also being attributed to the fact of 'staff turnover' in the 'sex-establishments'. The report also elaborates that new HIV & AIDS infection are due to the young people who are getting into this trade either as workers or clients. Rising experimentation with sex, drugs and alcohol by the young people that includes school children, is another major cause of concern for the Thai government. People engaged in 'indirect sex work' who operate in diverse, more difficult to regulate settings are now accounting for the sizeable portion of the sex-industry. As a result of which 'authorities are expressing an inability to monitor condom compliance in vastly increased direct/ indirect "sex-service establishments"' (Chhabra, 2007:108).

## Lessons for India

In India, one single, umbrella definition of sexual health free from socio-cultural, historical and personal contexts is probably impossible, given the tensions in definition of its root concepts of sexuality and health. In India, the single most frequently cited social obstacle to the control of HIV transmission and promotion of sexual health is a reluctance to talk explicitly about sex and sexual behaviour (Solomon et al., 1998; Bentley et al., 1998; George, 1997; Sethi, 2002). The publicly promoted image of Indian society is that of a highly moral cultural space marked by universal adherence to traditional values, in which girls and women are protected by fathers and husbands, young people remain 'uncorrupted' by knowledge of sexual matters and multiple sexual relationships do not exist (Sethi, 2002; Lambert, 2001). In this hegemonic discourse, sex is understood as a private act that can occur appropriately only with a legitimate marital relationship, and even there the sexual dimension of such relationships should remain as far as possible unacknowledged to the wider family and others. Commensurate with these understandings, attempts to introduce sex education in school and colleges in the wake of HIV epidemic have met with considerable resistance from concerned parents and religiously and politically conservative organisations. The public representation of 'traditional' Indian culture is counter-posed in dominant popular conceptions against that of the West as inherently degenerate and immoral, most specifically with respect to sexual intimacy with multiple partners and familial instability. The continual introduction of Western products in the form of clothes, music, consumer items and most importantly films and television, are seen in conservative circles as potentially destabilising influences that threaten to corrupt the moral standards of younger Indians. The threat of HIV is conceptually allied with these foreign influences. The associations have also created problems with respect to the official acceptance of the reality, and potential social and economic impact of the HIV epidemic in India. The relevance of other countries' experiences of the epidemic to the Indian context has also been questioned (Panda, 2002), as has the wisdom of adopting externally developed international strategies for HIV prevention and sexual health promotion, that are seen as imposed in disregard of local cultural values and social norms (Lambert, 2001). In the context of the international public health focus on sexual health and reproductive health (including HIV prevention), emphasis has often been placed on the need for research to elicit local understandings and vocabularies relating to sexual activity, sexuality, symptoms of sexually transmitted and reproductive tract infections and so forth, for use in the design of context-appropriate, and hence putatively more effective preventive communication interventions (Lambert, 1998). A few of the learnings for India from the above-mentioned countries are:

a  **Sexual health definition.** The world over there is no agreed definition of sexual health. The only available definition is that of the World Health Organisation. This definition cannot be applied universally as it might differ in different cultural/religious situations. None of the countries discussed above has come up with a definition that is relevant to the populace of the country. Finland and the Netherlands have attempted to come up with a definition on sexual health. India still emulates the WHO's definition of sexual health. But sooner or later it will have to devise a definition on sexual health that reflects the diversified realities of the country.

b  **Age for sexual debut.** Another important issue is that there is no uniform accepted age for sexual debut for young people. Though WHO and ILO consider age of 15 as the point from when they can start working, most countries consider 18 to be the age for issue of driving licences, juvenile justice or for sale of liquor. Countries like Uganda and Lesotho have been attempting to make 18 as a legal age at which girls can get married. But these countries do not specify it as an age for sexual debut, thereby promoting abstinence amongst the youth till they attain the age of 18. Swaziland had banned girls under 18 from sex, but it cannot be an indicator for sexual debut. Sex education can be targeted at them at an appropriate age.

c   **Contraceptive services and sex education.** Medical support to the population in India is relegated to only free distribution of condoms. Other contraceptive services are provided at cost in the government sector and at exorbitant cost in private hospitals. In many cities it is very common to find 'promotional ads' of doctors in public places offering to perform abortion at a premium. Whereas in the Netherlands and Finland most of the contraceptive services are provided free of cost and contraceptive education is part of the school curriculum. Such contraceptive education is missing in India. Contraception is promoted in India as a measure for married women, but campaigns rarely target unmarried women. Condoms also are promoted as a tool for preventing STDs in men, but discussions about unwanted pregnancy are uncommon. India in the current scenario needs to understand the sexual health needs of the population considering the diversity of culture, customs and practices.

d   **Drawbacks of ABCD approach and media campaigns.** After the advent of HIV & AIDS, demanding restraint amongst the population has become much tougher given the cultural background in India as elsewhere. Most of the campaigns have ingrained moral values in them, which those in the developed nations have not. Moreover, developed nations have not made any demands for abstinence from the youth but have sought to empower them to make responsible decisions regarding their own sexual health. Even public health research inputs are given by well-trained sex educators, a profession that is not very visible in India. India can think of low cost and easily accessible services of contraceptives and other related healthcare facilities under health insurance schemes. The initial sexual health messages were scary and vilifying in India. The same can also be observed in the case of Uganda, Lesotho, Finland and Swaziland. Over a period, sexual health messages started getting concentrated around morality. Thus, the ABCD (abstinence from sex, behaviour change and condom use/drugs) approach became prominent in the developing nations. This had a far-reaching effect on the sexual health patterns and behaviour of the masses. In a sense, the state started playing a major part in 'dictating' the norms for sexual behaviour (see the section on the ABCD approach and the moralisation of HIV & AIDS campaign in Chapter 4). In developed nations, media considers sexual health as a public agenda and plays a constructive role in providing information that caters to the needs of its population. The campaigns in developed nations also avoid moralistic approach on the issue of sexual health. At the same time, India is yet to come up with a comprehensive sexual health policy document, like in other countries. Countries like Uganda and Lesotho have evolved their own sexual health communication policy documents.

## Notes

1 www.rivm.nl/Images/24_Epidemiology_HIV%20estimate%20NL_tcm4-64705.pdf accessed on 09/01/2012.
2 www.womenfitness.net/news/womens_health/HIV_AIDS.htm accessed on 14/01/2013.
3 www.globalpost.com/dispatch/news/health/120704/swaziland-hiv-aids-adult-circum cision-campaign accessed on 16/01/2012.

# 4   HIV & AIDS messages
## Social construction of sexual health in India

Social constructionism examines how individuals and groups contribute to producing perceived social reality and knowledge (Berger & Luckmann, 1966). One of the most important intellectual foundations of the social construction perspective is social problems theory and research from the 1960s and 1970s. Scholars in this tradition asserted that what comes to be identified as deviant behaviour or a social problem is not 'given', but rather is conferred within a particular social context and in response to successful 'claims making' and 'moral entrepreneurialism' by social groups (Spector & Kitsuse (1977) as cited in Conrad & Barker, 2010:68). This is what could be observed in the context of HIV & AIDS, which started as an issue that needed to be addressed in the realm of medicine and later on came to be seen as an issue of morals and 'deviant' behaviours of the population. This chapter studies how sexual health is socially constructed through HIV & AIDS messages in India. In the context of HIV & AIDS, the social construction specifically refers to several themes: the cultural meaning of HIV & AIDS as an illness that is not derived from the nature of the disease and one that shapes the society's overall response to the epidemic. The illness experience can also be situated and constructed in the interplay of various social factors, which also refers to how people understand and communicate their illness in the daily context; and the medical knowledge as constructed and developed by policy interests.

This section considers Polgar's (1996) Social Constructions Model of Sexual Health (shown in Table 3.1). As stated, the medical model examines AIDS as a disease from a scientific and biomedical perspective; the epidemic model explains AIDS in terms of its transmission and prevention within a socio-cultural context; the organisational models target the issues and problems within health administrations and organisations; the moral model interprets AIDS from religious beliefs and perceptions; and the political model focuses on the state's political agenda. Each of the constructs is supported by the state, which frames the inherent problems and responses to HIV & AIDS. In turn it creates the dominant metaphors and symbols that guide the entire strategic approach on the epidemic. The National AIDS Control Organisation (NACO) in India did not follow any definite theoretical model for social construction of HIV in India but was guided by the theories that evolved at the international level.

## Medical model

### Depicting Human Immunodeficiency Virus (HIV)

The first and foremost discourse on HIV & AIDS is biomedical. A rational and scientific thought process was engaged as the deliberate effort to educate the masses about the virus. This was the most formidable task for the Government of India. In the context of other epidemics, this had an 'external' factor upon which the entire campaign was run. For instance, for malaria or filaria it was a 'mosquito' around which the entire programme was strategised. But for HIV, it was a virus that could only be seen under clinical conditions. It became a challenge for the Government of India to diagram it and educate the people about the virus. The Government of India's HIV & AIDS policies lay huge emphasis on such bio-medical knowledge imported from the West. This became very much evident in the language, prescriptions, and descriptions on how it was constructed for consumption by the masses during NACP-I (1992–99). This was again followed by the use of other medical terms such as asymptomatic period, immune system, symptoms, and severe infections. HIV & AIDS in the NACP-I (1992–99) was presented as a medical condition. The language and construction of sentences in the posters was in conventional biomedical mode where the epidemic was described in the standard language of disease: cause, symptom, treatment, prevention, infection/infected, transmitted, and precautions. This may be because the very nature of the epidemic can be said to be constructed through the discourses of medicine and science that was imported from the West; after all, the name HIV & AIDS in part constructs the epidemic and helps make it intelligible. Biomedical discourse is characterised with its overly mechanistic attributes. Proponents of this discourse believe that biomedical practitioners which include doctors, nurses and other para-medical staff view the body as an object to be 'repaired'. According to mainstream medical discourse propagated during the NACP-I, HIV infection will always lead to AIDS and ultimately death without question. Metaphors like *sazaa* (punishment), *mazaa* (pleasure) and *mardangi* (masculinity) went onto become the prominent metaphors that constructed the virus and the whole gamut of issues around it.

Contrary to popular belief, many people have lived healthy, productive lives with HIV & AIDS since the onset of the epidemic—with the help of alternative methods. Many continue to do so, with or without the assistance of pharmaceuticals. Throughout the history of the epidemic, many substances and treatments have proved highly efficacious in providing relief and restoring the immune system. This information was never clearly visible in the mainstream media or made available through medical support systems. Unfortunately, alternative treatments were highly suppressed by the medical (Western) establishment that portrayed HIV & AIDS as a 'guaranteed' death sentence. This aspect led to the rise of stigma and discrimination amongst the population. In parallel, another form of health system arose in the forms of quacks and herbal-based treatments. The sexual health communication material developed and disseminated by the NACO and the various State AIDS Control Societies presented such scientifically constructed representations of HIV during the NACP-I, which challenged the assumption of a single authoritative truth typical of modernism. This position allowed for a critical stance towards taken-for-granted knowledge and an understanding that knowledge is historically and culturally specific (Burr, 1995). In the book *AIDS: The Burdens of History,* Fee and Fox (1988:3) compiled articles concerning the 'burden' of AIDS virus as essentially medico-moral, which 'offer a more thorough reading of the history of infectious diseases', discussing the continuities and differences of medical and social responses to AIDS virus compared with previous epidemics. The campaigns carried out by NACO in NACP-I were mostly on and about the virus and the epidemic, contributing to the social panic that followed, which in turn led to hasty demands for impossible cures in a short period of time. The only recourse around the world was to find a 'miracle drug' that eliminates the virulent pathogen known as 'HIV'. Thus, in order to fully understand this epidemic's social and individual impact, a medico-moral orientation focusing on individual and group behaviours was far from sufficient, and the larger political and social environment with its symbolic resonances had to be taken into account in research enquiries. Messages brought out initially during the NACP-I presented a scientific representation of the Human Immunodeficiency Virus (HIV). It can be construed as a very ambitious attempt by the state to depict and inform the people about how the virus actually looks albeit under clinical conditions. At the same time, it also tried to educate the people by expanding the HIV & AIDS abbreviation but did not detail what it actually meant. It also did not describe how the immune system falls prey to the virus. It also failed to discuss more on how the virus affects the body. Thus, this kind of biomedical narrative really constructed HIV & AIDS as a deadly 'disease'.

### Depicting Acquired Immune Deficiency Syndrome (AIDS)

Every human being has an inbuilt immune system that fights any foreign element that invades it. An inept failure of this immune system causes a huge problem for the human body. The Human Immunodeficiency Virus invades this immune system and causes Acquired Immune Deficiency Syndrome (AIDS). For example, if a person gets affected by common cold after having got infected by the virus, the human body fails to guard against it because the immune system has become deficient. This phenomenon is called Acquired Immune Deficiency Syndrome (AIDS). Therefore, it can be clearly inferred that HIV & AIDS got around as a 'disease', which is 'deadly', but not as an immune deficiency syndrome. This can be attributed to the fact, that people were not so 'scientifically informed' to know AIDS in simple terms. Another factor can also be that medical model constructed it in technical terms. Thereby, the people understood AIDS in medical terms and as a 'disease' because the information primarily came from the doctors. The initial posters on HIV & AIDS prominently portrayed doctors talking about HIV & AIDs. Thereby, was seen as a medical problem. The messages built around this concept socially constructed this phenomenon. Most of the campaigns were borrowed from the West in doing this. Posters carried messages on 'How the virus spreads and how it does not spread'—became an integral part of the social construction of AIDS in the initial days. The Government of India was reasonably comfortable while telling the people how it did not spread, but had a tough time talking about the sexual route of transmission. For some time, it talked about the transmission of virus through blood and injecting needles (detailed later). But talking about sex and the sexual route was still a strict no-no. The general perception was that as a conservative, close-knit, and family-oriented society, it is near impossible for Indians to get infected by the virus. The government felt that unprotected sex could only be the indulgence of people who are 'deviant' in their sexual behaviours, which is a rarity in India. But later on, this hypothesis proved wrong for which the Government of India had to spend a lot of money to raise the awareness levels in the people that HIV & AIDS can affect anyone unmindful of the sexual orientation or behaviours.

### Constructing HIV & AIDS as THE disease

It needs to be mentioned here that the population was segregated into risky and not-affected by the agencies that were responsible for designing communication messages. Because AIDS, unlike some other diseases, cannot be controlled by public health strategies such as improvement of sanitation or disinfecting facilities, one is compelled to explain it in other terms to make an effect on the psyche of the population. One such approach forces people to make informed decisions on their sexual health practices. Communication campaigns, through posters, TV, radio, teaser ads, exhibition panels, comic strips etc. internalise and promoted state discourses of normative sexual health. Discourses on normative sexual health, particularly emanating from authority structures, typically identify not only the source of 'disease'—AIDS –but also the mindset of the people who conceive the messages. Firstly, there was much debate on the cause of AIDS and a framework was established for explaining the progression of the disease. Again, the device directed attention away from the socio-cultural factors that are responsible for the spread of AIDS within the country. The state's discourse framed the struggle against AIDS in the language of war, a battle that needs to be won with messages such as *Vijay ki tayyari (*Preparation for victory). This is not surprising. We know that medicine frequently draws on the metaphor of the battlefield. Posters on 'war on germs', for instance, are common in toothpaste advertisements. NACO's posters were also framed in the language of war and battle. The posters reveal the language of war, where AIDS is constructed as an enemy that needs to be defeated. Few posters also used red colour prominently while depicting AIDS. Messages such 'AIDS does not end life' depicted in red colour instilled danger or fear in the population.

The first HIV & AIDS case was diagnosed in 1986 and National AIDS Control Programme-I, was set up. Its campaign focus was on the medical model that described HIV scientifically, in terms of compromised immune system, opportunistic infections, treatment, and care. National AIDS Control Organisation (NACO) and the various State AIDS Control Societies focused on this aspect extensively. This phase re-positioned (after the Population Control Programme) and attempted to popularise the use of condoms by increasing their availability and quality. A social marketing approach was adopted to promote and distribute condoms through extensive use of market-based consumer needs, preferences, and perceptions. Condoms were branded, advertised extensively and the supply outlets were increased for easy availability. Vendors were provided with low-priced condoms and were encouraged to sell at higher prices. Small shopkeepers as well as outreach workers were allowed to keep a share of the profit for themselves. Thus, such kinds of efforts emphasised and socially constructed HIV & AIDS as a 'disease' that needs to be 'controlled' by the use of 'tools' such as condoms. The widespread promotion of condoms led to a general perception that any kind of sexual relationship is safe. The virus in such manner got constructed as a war that only can be won only by condom (Kumar, 2000).

### Depiction of blood donation as gift of life

The easiest way of informing the people about HIV & AIDS without worrying about inherent cultural taboos was blood donation. Shortly after the first AIDS case in 1986, the Government of India established a National AIDS Control Programme (NACP) that was managed by a small unit within the Ministry of Health and Family Welfare. The programme's principal activity was then limited to monitoring HIV infection rates among risk populations in select urban areas. In 1991, the strategy was revised to focus on blood safety, prevention among high-risk populations, raising awareness in the general population, and improving surveillance. A semi-autonomous body, the National AIDS Control Organisation (NACO), was established under the Ministry of Health and Family Welfare to implement this programme. This 'first phase' of the National AIDS Control Programme lasted from 1992–99. It focused on initiating a national commitment, increasing awareness, and addressing blood safety. It achieved some of its objectives, including increased awareness. During this phase, professional blood donations were banned by law. Screening of donated blood became almost universal by the end of this phase. By 1999, the programme had also established a decentralised mechanism to facilitate effective state-level responses, although substantial variation continued to exist in the level of commitment and capacity among states. Blood donation, after the rise of the epidemic, was constructed as an activity undertaken by someone like a Superman or something done by tough (men), smart (girls), and sensible people. Such kind of posters again played into the stereotypical understanding of gender, where men are 'tough' and women are 'smart'. This type of campaign was followed for a long time in India, where men ultimately became the valiant saviour for protecting a 'weak' woman from the virus. Blood donation was also constructed as an activity of *jeevan daan* (divine experience) or as a *vardaan* (boon).

The entire blood collection, processing, storage, and distribution systems were revamped in 1996 after a judgement by the Supreme Court. This led to establishment of national and state blood transfusion councils and formulation of National Blood Transfusion Policy (NACO, 2003). An action plan for blood safety (NACO, 2003a) was also formulated and guidelines were issued on aspects of blood donation, testing, and storage and it was made mandatory for the blood banks to obtain licences. Zonal blood banks were set up and modernised by the funds provided by the National AIDS Control Programme. In order to reduce the risk of HIV through unsafe blood from professional blood donors, professional blood donation was banned. Component segregation units were set up to split a single unit of blood into several components at big blood banks. This segregated blood units were given to the patients who required such components (Kumar, 2000).

### Depiction of HIV & AIDS through colour

The extensive use of the colour red was prominent during all the phases of National AIDS Control Programme (NACP) in India. The red ribbon that went on to signify the persistent efforts undertaken upon HIV & AIDS the world over is one such example. One reason could be that it derived its colour from the colour of the blood cells—DNA. Extensive use of the colour red also led to fear, stigma, and as a symbol of danger in the larger population. Baron Peter Piot, the founding executive director states in the World Alzheimer Report (2012:18):

> What we must learn from the AIDS movement is that it takes a lot of work, coalition-building, campaigning and lobbying to change attitudes. Much time and effort were spent trying to overcome bureaucracy and official denial—and stigma attached to AIDS victims. The red ribbon effectively turned this stigma into a powerful symbol for a worldwide movement. The activists were vital in putting moral and political pressure on governments to act both locally and globally.

HIV or AIDS or related metaphors were prominently displayed in red in almost all the posters, where the colour red has been used extensively that further led to stigma and discrimination about HIV & AIDS in India.

Greater efforts were needed again from the government to shed the stigma and eliminate discrimination in the later stages. The use of the colour red was responsible for much greater investment of resources in tackling HIV & AIDS.

### Interpreting the medical model's discourse

After discussions with key people involved in the communication campaigns of this period, it was observed that a number of people who led the earliest discourse on HIV & AIDS in this phase were doctors. It was obvious where the interests lay for them. HIV being a biomedical issue and the 'foreign' tag that came along with it, the 'foreign' approach to the epidemic drove the strategy during the NACP-I phase. The Government of India laid greater emphasis on tackling the problem in a clinical or scientific manner. It was a clinical problem, the government thought it could be only handled by the clinicians. The way you trust the army in tackling terrorists, the same also applied to the HIV epidemic as well. HIV is a terrorist, and the doctors the army. If we examine this discourse closely, we can observe that most of the graphics used in the posters for spreading awareness were Western. For instance, shaking of hands, computers, cups, saucers and spoon, as well as the Western toilets signified the Western influence on information dissemination. It can also be presumed that posters got developed in the West and were brought into India, and only the illustrations were changed to suit the local contexts. Moreover, the government was initially in a denial mode. The media were also looked at with skepticism. It was thought that media spread 'morally wrong' and 'dangerous information'. Therefore, anything on the media about HIV & AIDS was frowned upon. There were also no studies done on communication or needs analysis in the initial period. As a result of which, wrong programmes were conceived and delivered which led to stigma and discrimination. This proved to be a challenge for the policymakers in the later years.

> Communication was always seen as 'art work' and printing charges by the National AIDS Control Organisation (NACO). A limited budget was allocated for communication activities. There was no proper research or planning, and neither were any efforts made for development of communication material. Getting approval from the government was also a Herculean task for the programme managers at NACO during the initial stages of the programme. At one stage, it was very difficult to get the messages approved by the government because talking about HIV & AIDS was a forbidden topic, at least in India
>
> (Interview: Technical specialist-STD, NACO)

Subtle political statements of 'abstinence' and 'single-partner sex' also started emanating from different quarters, be it the right-wing political class, religious leaders, or simply from the families. The posters during the NACP-I generally talked about *'unprotected sex* with an infected person'. But nowhere does the state tell its citizens about what is 'unprotected' and 'infected'. That's because it was forbidden to talk about sex and sexuality so boldly. Inputs or briefs were given by the doctors and, sometimes, by the support staff of NACO to the advertising agencies who were developing the communication material. It can be deduced that the inherent understanding and perceptions of people working at NACO also played a significant role on how the brief was passed on. The 'art work' people also had limited knowledge, to which the support staff and the doctors fed their own understanding and beliefs of sex, sexuality, and normative sex practices. Thus, the messages that got disseminated to the masses were routed through particular social constructions of sexuality.

*Youn sambandh* (sexual relationships) and *sammbhog* (coitus) could not be understood by many people in North India for a long time. This could have emanated from a person who reads too much into the messages spread by the quacks who operate in North India, who cure 'sex' problems (Interview: M & E expert, NACO). With no established health mechanism to cater to the communication needs of the people regarding HIV & AIDS, the majority of the populace depended on quacks for information. They became the substitutes for the peer group. This again compounded the problems of the government; they had to segregate and bring back the population, which was approaching quacks and instil confidence in them with renewed efforts; and provide health systems that cater to them exclusively on HIV & AIDS. Confidentiality and secrecy was another major area on which the government had to do a lot of campaigning. Mainstream films in the initial years of HIV & AIDS in India also played a malicious role for the further spread of stigma and discrimination amongst the general population (Ingle & Vemula, 2012). HIV & AIDS was depicted in a comic manner in films in India. Many films have shown comedians ridicule AIDS as a no-cure disease and as a death warrant. As a result of which, the masses took it as truth and treated it as a part of reality. As the epidemic progressed, the government's main focus shifted to sex and sexuality while addressing HIV & AIDS. The discussion on blood and blood donation and messages targeted at blood donors was not so prominent during NACP-II and III but was given equal importance during both the phases. But still, in the initial years talking about blood donation was the safest way for the government, without it being seen as trespassing on the sensitive issue of sex and sexuality. It can be observed that the majority of the posters during this phase were on blood and blood donation. Blood screening and testing became the mainstay for the Government of India.

Later on, sexual health as a concept was brought in by the government as a soft term to discuss HIV & AIDS. This approach helped the policymakers discuss in explicit terms, sex and sexuality. The depiction and perception of the virus and its association with a 'disease' that's incurable became vociferous during the NACP-II and III. A major response to HIV & AIDS was the huge investments being made in research testing and treatment. India also became a member country for the worldwide research that was carried out for HIV & AIDS vaccine. Though, a costly treatment was available in the developed countries that delayed the onset of the virus, it was not affordable in India. India started making efforts towards cost-effective drug therapy for the infected patients as part of vaccination and cure.

## Epidemic model

The AIDS epidemic is not only shaped by powerful biological forces, but also by behavioural, social, and cultural factors. There is substantial evidence in India where the majority of sexual health communication campaigns focused on addressing the issue based on such factors. In the early 1980s, the 'cultural factors' first mobilised around a moral focus on deviant sexuality; official discourse, however, quickly moved on to recognise that the danger was not confined to deviant sexual behaviour but in fact was found everywhere. This reaction, which led to generalised panic, has brought about a contradictory response by the state: on the one hand, an increased commitment to moral policing (discussed in next section on moral models), and on the other, attempts to liberalise the legislative regime in an effort to establish the full extent of the epidemic. The epidemic model is guided by the behavioural patterns of any culture towards a social problem. Risk behaviours and the dependant health services are located as the epicenters of the epidemic model. The major response for this model is on public education and prevention campaigns. The Government of India's primary focus in NACP-II was on prevention efforts on sexually transmitted diseases (STDs). It was stated that, if a person protected herself/himself from STDs (usage of condom by males), they would ultimately protect themselves from HIV. Thereby, STD became another jargon that was added to the international sexual health vocabulary.

By the early 1990s, the understanding of AIDS as merely a 'biomedical problem' has been changed to that of a psychological, social, and political problem responding to the perspective emanating from HIV & AIDS research. The exclusive medical definition of AIDS has drawn widespread criticism, for linking AIDS to the rational-scientific worldview which 'is characterised by its detached and respectful attitude towards facts, its efforts at objectivity, and its interpretation of the givens of nature, including diseases, as data to be studied, explained, and reduced to more basic phenomena' (Keinston 1989:2). Keinston further proposes two ways in which AIDS is socially constructed: first, it is socially constructed in the sense that for any disease we assign a meaning to the condition, in a broader framework of traditional meanings, appealing metaphors, and convincing theories; second, the symptoms of the disease are socially constructed since they grow out of personal, ecological, social, cultural, and historical contexts. Social construction of AIDS through different symbolic frameworks, asserts AIDS as a 'disease', which is a characteristically a modern construction and the misleading use of metaphors of 'war', 'crisis', and 'plague' inspire false hopes of the rapid 'conquest' of this condition and paralysing fears of the imminent catastrophe (Keinston, 1989:19–22). The language used in talking about HIV & AIDS in the 1980s largely focused on people dying from it rather than on people living with it.

### Construction of risk and risk behaviour

Risk behaviour is a scientific classification of social behaviour derived from epidemiological analysis or 'risk assessment', the basis of which is not immediately obvious to the public. Therefore, people tend to rely on intuitive judgments (risk perceptions) about the hazards in their lives (Slovic, 1987). Risk, on the one hand refers to the possibility of loss or injury and, on the other could be threatening or dangerous elements or factors. Risk can, therefore, be perceived both as an internal property, as harm occurring to the self that is not overtly the result of the external agents, or as derived from external forces. The NACO's perception about risk reduction through sexual health messages suggests a paradigm shift that involves reduction in risk exposure but not in harm reduction during exposure. This approach eventually required a fundamental strategic shift from targeted interventions among high-risk groups to community-based strategies. The NACP-II & III focused on this perspective, and its messages were more community specific rather than being individualist. This would entail deferring to people's innate wisdom to arrive at appropriate solutions, together with programmatic inputs concentrated on instituting primary preventive interventions against causative factors identified by the people so that exposure to the risks or behaviour in question is tackled together with effective, appropriate information and counselling, including secondary preventive measures like condoms (Chhabra, 2007:106).

The National IEC/BCC Strategic Framework for HIV & AIDS Programme (2004:6) clearly outlined that the specificity of the audience has been an issue in the previous communication efforts. The issue of greater and sometimes excessive focus on high-risk core groups sometimes lead to the belief that I am 'normal' and 'regular person' and 'therefore not at risk'. The over-targeting of an audience or a group and non-targeting of another also lead to unintended consequences and added to stigma and discrimination. Care had to be taken so that audience segmentation would not lead to 'labeling'. The focus of this strategic framework was on the general population. The desirable and feasible behaviours are delay of sexual activity (discussed in empowering the young through sexual health messages), not indulging in multi-partner sex, not sharing needles, not taking HIV-infected blood, getting oneself checked for HIV, availing the services for STIs and not stigmatising and discriminating against People Living with HIV & AIDS. The high-risk population got addressed with messages upon 'safety' in either the form of a condom or in the form of using clean needles or syringes. The 'I decide' campaign of NACO posited this type of strategic shift adopted by the state, while socially constructing HIV & AIDS as the epidemic.

Risk can be something you do to yourself (taking risks) or something done to you. 'I am in Control'—posters of NACO clearly illustrated that the person is aware what is signified by risk behaviour. HIV education programmes in India have focused on the personal responsibility model of risk in their risk-reduction messages. Therefore, if individuals participate in certain behaviours, they put themselves at risk of contracting HIV and getting AIDS. While this approach appears to be effective in encouraging individuals to be aware of the potential consequences of their actions and to take responsibility for changing their behaviour to protect themselves, it fails to address adequately the other aspect of HIV risk: that one's partner may constitute a threat to one's health and life. By focusing on risk behaviours, contemporary risk reduction campaigns convey the impression that behaviours can be 'targeted for change', apart from the relationships in which they occur. What is meant by 'risky behaviours' is, in reality, risky relationships, and from the point of view of those to whom these messages are directed, this is at once more meaningful and more threatening. It is threatening because sex is a socially symbolic act and because the hazard presented by participation in these sexual relationships is contracting an STD. Most health communication campaigns invoke the idea of risk, i.e. risks to people and societal risks. The concept of risk has been at the focus of contemporary thinking in most of the health communication campaigns in India as well as all round the world. Messages discussed about the *laingik jeevan* (sex life) and the issues concerned with it. One such poster urged the audience to come to a photo exhibition and learn what constituted 'risk' in 'sex life'. Observations have been made on the traditional cultures that do not have a concept of risk, but it is considered as a concept associated with modern industrialised civilisation, embodying ideas about controlling or conquering the future (Giddens, 1999). While experts can assess the likelihood and magnitude of a given risk, the public understanding of a given risk takes on specific meanings through our own cultural practices (Adams, 1995). The entire discourse on risk behaviour initially focused more on injected needles and drug abuse. Few of the posters also raised the issue of *guptang (*secret organs) and motivated the audience to learn about sexually transmitted diseases and its treatment. Posters also attempted to address the various myths surrounding STDs, such as they cannot subside by just hiding them (*chupane se*), washing of 'secret organs' with lemon/soda/petrol (*nimbu, soda ya petrol se dhone se*), having sex with a virgin girl (*kunwari ladki ke saath sambhog karne se*). The messages developed during the NACP-I, accepted HIV & AIDS as an epidemic present in a size that was a cause of concern and that needed measures taken on an urgent basis. The messages developed during this phase yielded its results in terms of dissemination of information related to the routes of transmission and modes of prevention. The messages focused on seeing the epidemic as a concentrated one whose primary focus was on addressing the high-risk behaviour of the population. Several states in India were also selected on the basis of high prevalence and messages were developed to address the 'risk population' of these states.

### Depiction of injecting drug users

Although injecting drug use was known to be prevalent in many major cities of India during the NACP-I, the problem of HIV was extensively investigated in North East India and in cities such as Chennai, Kolkata, and Delhi. Ironically, the majority of the posters that were conceived during this phase came from the North East India, which talked about care and prevention efforts regarding drug abuse. The 'I Decide' posters during that phase were an indicator of perception about North East Indian people being drug addicts, amongst the policymakers. The posters, thus, constructed a perception that a majority of the injecting drug users are primarily young males who live in the North East India in spite of the high level of awareness about the possibility of HIV transmission through sharing of needles routinely. A study among women in Manipur in 1997 revealed a high HIV prevalence of 57% among drug users compared to 20% among non-injecting drug users (Panda, 2002). A study in Chennai also reported multiple risk behaviours like exchanging money for sex or having sex with men among men who used illicit drugs. Thus, in addition to prevention of parenteral (injection of syringes) transmission, Government of India undertook measures like reducing availability of drugs, de-addiction programmes, education for safe injecting practices, and providing clean needles which was clubbed with prevention of sexual transmission of HIV by the policymakers in various drug-use settings (Go et al., 2003).

### Social construction of infection and transmission of HIV

Educating people about how HIV & AIDS prevention is complicated in India because of the number of major languages and hundreds of different dialects that are spoken among its population. This means that, although some HIV & AIDS prevention and education can be done at the national level, many of the efforts are best carried out at the state and local level. Each state has its own AIDS Prevention and Control Society, which carries out local initiatives with guidance from NACO. During the second stage of the government's National AIDS Control Programme (NACP-II, 1999–2006), which finished in March 2006, state AIDS Control Societies were granted funding for youth campaigns, blood safety checks, and HIV testing, among other things. Various public platforms were used to raise awareness of the epidemic—concerts, radio dramas, a voluntary blood donation day, and TV spots with a popular Indian film star. Messages were also conveyed to young people through schools. Teachers and peer educators were trained to teach about the subject, and students were educated through active learning sessions, including debates and role-play. There are many examples of how HIV prevention campaigns in India were tailored to the situations of different states and areas. In doing so, they sought to make an impact, particularly in rural areas where information is often lacking. Small-scale campaigns were often run or supported by NGOs in such areas, which were to play a vital role in informing people about HIV infections throughout India, particularly among high-risk groups that include women. In some cases, members of risk groups such as MSMs, CSWs, etc., formed their own organisations to respond to the epidemic. A national AIDS helpline (1097) was also launched. The government has however, funded a small number of national campaigns to spread awareness about HIV & AIDS to complement the local level initiatives. On World AIDS Day 2007, a train—the Red Ribbon Express was flagged off to reach most parts of the country (NACO, 2010). In 2009, counselling and training services, HIV testing, treatment of STDs as well as HIV & AIDS education and awareness were included as part of the 'Red Ribbon Express'. According to a mid-year report (2009) on the progress of the second round of the Red Ribbon Express, NACO estimated that 3.8 million people were reached in the first six months of the campaign. The NACO termed the response as 'overwhelming', with queues of people waiting to access the services a common sight and follow-up surveys indicated that knowledge of transmission routes of HIV and prevention methods increased significantly in the areas visited by the train. In general, this goes to support the study that when education is culturally specific and tailored to the unique issues and needs of the targeted community, it is more likely to lead to positive outcomes (Rokeach, 1969; Pitts et al., 1989; Yep, 1993; Bockting et al., 1999). Posters were brought out specifically at a later stage that described HIV (Human Immunodeficiency Virus) causes Acquired Immune Deficiency Syndrome (AIDS) and is a medical definition. Poster explicitly detailed graphic images about how the virus spreads by u*nprotected sex with an infected person.* Few posters also lay a background for the other concerns of the NACP-I, such as blood transfusion, sharing of contaminated needles, and infection from mother to child. The underlying message of such images can be read as people with 'deviant' behaviour will have 'unprotected sex' and will ultimately become an 'infected' person. The media, for instance, distinguished between 'normal' behaviour and 'deviant' behaviour, blaming 'imported' habits for HIV & AIDS and viewing foreigners as HIV carriers (Wolffers, 1997). The same is true in Indian context also. Traditionally, most Indian health officials and the healthcare establishments viewed HIV as a 'foreign' disease or an 'imported' infection, confined to people returning from foreign countries or port cities and to marginalised groups such as sex workers and drug users and unlikely to spread to the general population (Mitra, 2004). The media distinguished this aspect very clearly and played onto the psychology of the people. Images or films that got circulated during the initial days of the epidemic built on this perspective that HIV is 'foreign'—because they (in the West) have a 'gay' tradition, which is absent in India. The extensive efforts by NACO and the world bodies targeting sex workers as the 'carriers' also reinforced this 'foreign tag'.

NACO brought out posters to discuss about how the HIV does not spread. The graphics in such posters show things that cannot be identified with the poor or Indian living conditions— (cups/saucers, computers, and Western cisterns, etc.). Similar posters were also brought out by the Jharkhand AIDS Control Society (JACS) and Uttarakhand AIDS Control Society (UACS) to educate the people about the various modes of transmission of the virus in Hindi. At the same time, it also featured how the virus does not spread. All the posters developed by the NACO, UACS, and JACS used the same visuals as developed by the NACO, but only elaborated on the other aspects, such as AIDS does not spread if *we sit and live together* rather than *working together.* The English one just mentions *touch* but the Hindi one goes a step ahead and suggests that the virus does not spread through *social interaction.* The Hindi poster also states that HIV does not spread by the bite of a *mosquito or bed bug.* May be the message designers of Uttarakhand were focusing on the living conditions of the people of that region. The National IEC/BCC strategic framework for HIV & AIDS programme (2004) initiated on the core principles that complete and correct knowledge on the routes of transmission and modes of prevention. This new holistic and comprehensive communication approach focused on the four routes of transmission as discussed previously, with not just basic knowledge but accurate and complete information. These messages specifically focused on addressing the barriers in HIV & AIDS transmission.

The initial framework for AIDS was 'a rare cancer' (Sontag, 1991), with the concomitant discursive framework of waging war against such illness. As in the past, messages were designed for a 'fight or war' against cancer, in the same manner HIV & AIDS was also described. Messages clearly outlined that HIV & AIDS is an illness that need to be 'won over' (discussed in detail in HIV & AIDS and the Construction of war and victory section). A discourse of war as noted, described in ways how cancer is understood as a symbol of death and extinction, incorporating a fear of being overwhelmed by an image of decline, images about HIV & AIDS as a 'cancer' with 'guaranteed death' got constructed (Karpf, 1988; Williams & Miller, 1995). A discourse of war has been pervasive in the official health administration with respect to their approach to both cancer and HIV & AIDS (Sontag, 1991; Lupton, 1993; Brown et al., 1996). Information, education and prevention are presented as the weapons of choice in this battle. A central contribution regarding identification and control of HIV & AIDS is made by medical science resulting in a 'detective' discourse in which rational strategies of deduction and detection are adopted to locate the 'villains' responsible for the 'crime' and then to 'punish' them (Brown et al., 1996). While there are similarities in the war discourse of cancer and HIV & AIDS, there are also differences. Posters talk about two enemies that are to be defeated: a). *aneko se sambandh* (multi-partner sex) and *AIDs ko Nimantran* (invitation to AIDS). This invariably meant that 'multi-partner sex' definitely is an invitation to AIDS, and it can only be fought (*jung*) with a condom (*condom ke sang*).

Thus, the condom becomes a weapon that is needed to fight the virus. HIV & AIDS is understood to have a greater element of personal will or intention or a reflection of a deviant behaviour. Getting HIV & AIDS through a sexual practice, injecting drugs, or by sharing needles is thought to be more intentional and therefore deserving of more blame (Sontag, 1991). Such kind of 'blame-centric' (deviant) activities of the population laid a formidable ground for stigma and discrimination.

### Dealing with social discrimination and stigma discourse

Jonathan Mann, 1987 as cited in ICMR (2002:1–2) stressed on three phases on the progression of the disease:

1   The epidemic of HIV infection that enters into a society silently and develops over many years without being widely perceived or understood.
2   The epidemic of AIDS itself, the syndrome of infectious diseases that can occur because of HIV infection but typically after a delay of many years.
3   The epidemic of social, cultural, economic and political responses to HIV & AIDS, which is characterised by exceptionally high levels of stigma, discrimination and collective denial.

In the year 2000, UNAIDS identified stigma as a 'continuing challenge' that prevents concerted action at community, national and global levels. HIV & AIDS-related stigma and discrimination also interact with pre-existing fears about contagion and disease (ICMR, 2002). NACO's poster to break such stigma can be seen on one such where it tried to address the concerns through images of a mother-in-law and a daughter-in-law. The poster brought out the cultural facet out in open whilst talking about HIV infection and stigma associated with it. A mother-in-law talking frankly about the 'opportunistic infection' that her *bahu* (daughter-in-law) has contracted, and about which she is comfortable. Such campaign attempted to venture into a relationship that was seldom talked about in the past. Such posters also came up when there were instances reported, of a daughter-in-law who was thrown out of her house, because she was infected by the virus. Though facts state that the woman may have contracted the virus from the husband who stays away from the family and may have contracted the virus elsewhere (unprotected sex). Thereby the mother-in-law attempts to dispel the stigma associated with it through such posters. A description of stigma incorporates an acknowledgement of cultural values: it is a depiction of life as an individual within the social or cultural milieu. In the context of HIV & AIDS, the stigma is associated with the devastating medical progression of opportunistic infection, moral transgressions in the context of both homosexual and heterosexual relationships and afflictions transmitted through the notions of risky group as opposed to risky behaviour. These descriptions led to the notions of 'us' and 'them', where the latter are stigmatised through the values and attitudes based on moral judgments (ICMR, 2002). Another such poster elucidates this fact and attempts to dispel the stigma and discrimination surrounding HIV & AIDS. *Jiyo aur Jeeno do (* Live and let live) was an effort by the government. Images were circulated about a village setting where the panchayat, tries to destigmatise the village about an HIV & AIDS infected person, after hearing it from a doctor.

The earlier metaphors of HIV & AIDS such as death, horror, guilt, shame further intensified, reinforcing and legitimising stigma and discrimination (Gilmore & Somerville, 1994; Aggleton et al., 2003; Ogden et al., 1999). Continuous exposure to half-baked information and incomplete messages reinforced the image in people's minds that it is a life-threatening disease that would result in death if contracted. Various metaphors that came up due to HIV & AIDS also contributed to the perception of HIV & AIDS as a disease that affects 'others', who are already stigmatised because of their 'deviant sexual behaviour', and socio-economic status (Malcolm et al., 1998; Daniel & Parker, 1993). This perception amongst certain sections of the population got into the denial mode that they personally could be at risk or affected as compared to the people with deviant sexual behaviours. Messages also built in the perspective of 'positive' and 'special' which invariably lead to the perception that only the negative (sexually deviant people) should express themselves as being positive. It does not in any manner seclude people who might have got infected other than through the sexual intercourse mode. Moreover, because HIV & AIDS campaigns are invariably associated with marginalised behaviours and groups, the campaigns also assumed blindly that all the HIV & AIDS infected persons are from the marginalised groups that led to further stigmatisation of the people affected by it. For example, in some settings, men feared revealing their HIV status because it will be assumed that either they are homosexual or have a deviant behaviour. Similarly, women also feared revealing their serostatus because they may be labelled as 'promiscuous' or as sex workers and stigmatised as such. HIV & AIDS worsens the situations and increases the vulnerability of the individuals and groups who are already oppressed and marginalised due to the various factors in the society that ultimately increases their chances of vulnerability. As a result of which this section of the population who are marginalised neither have the resources to counter the infection nor is able to ward off the social stigma attached with the virus (Parker & Aggleton, 2002). Many countries had also during the same time put restrictions on international travel and were vociferous in demanding a certification from foreign travelers/migrants about their HIV status. This approach was another kind of discrimination against the people affected by HIV & AIDS (Solon & Barrazo, 1993). Some countries even restricted the entry of People Living with HIV & AIDS (PLWHA) carrying medical drugs, which led to international ramifications that further stigmatised the disease. There were many reports of deportation of people when found to be HIV-positive (Duckett & Orkin 1989; Malcolm et al., 1998). Attempts were made to dispel the stigma surrounding the virus and calls for attention to the people who are infected with the virus *Pyar de tiraskar nahin* (Shower love on AIDS infected person) and *dur rahein AIDS se na ki AIDS grast vyakti se* (stay away from AIDS but not from an AIDS infected person). Stigma and discrimination were countered and fought back by the Government of India by such approaches where it again constructs its approach as a fight (*Ladai*) against the virus.

### Construction of HIV & AIDS as the social disease

'AIDS is infectious but also a social disease. The ramification of HIV & AIDS has extended far beyond traditional medical interest' (Velimirovic, 1987 as cited in Temu et al., 2008:213). Although a cure or vaccine is yet to be found, the rapid pace at which knowledge about the dynamics of the disease accumulated is without precedent. HIV & AIDS as a disease is affecting complex social structures in general, and health structures in particular. HIV is also shaping the future attitudes, values and morals that cannot be delineated with any degree of precision the disease progresses now and into the next century.

The National AIDS Prevention and Control Policy (NACO, 2002:5) document of the Government of India acknowledges that HIV & AIDS is not merely a public health challenge, it is also a political and social challenge. Change in behaviour will not occur without a significant change in social and political environment. Unequal gender and power relations, taboos to frank and open communication about sexual health, and stigma and discrimination are particularly significant obstacles. The document underlines the fact that there is still inadequate understanding of the serious implications of the disease among the legislators, political, social and religious leaders, bureaucracy and media. It also acknowledges the fact that 'there is serious information gap about the causes of spread of the disease among a large number of medical and paramedical personnel' (NACO, 2002:10). The National IEC/BCC Strategic Framework for HIV & AIDS Programme (NACO, 2004) describes messages during NACP-I as the first generation of messages that focused on 'safety' and actually translated them into secondary behaviour change (e.g. use of condoms) and harm or risk reduction activities. The second generation of messages (NACP-II) needed to build on the first generation of messages focusing primarily on prevention. The campaign focus shifted onto primary behaviour change, risk perception enhancement and focus on the worth of a life. Care, support and treatment and access and utilisation of the health system became key focus areas for messages during the second-generation messages. Messages also provided information on additional counselling and voluntary testing. Normalisation of the epidemic was the underlying theme for the second generation of messages developed by the National AIDS Control Organisation. These problems created polarisation among public, politicians, press and also among physicians on how to approach the vexatious concept of HIV & AIDS. They got divided around the entire debate on appropriate cultural approaches to fight the epidemic. NACP-IV was launched in April 2012, with the vision that, by 2020, the number of HIV infected people in India, would gradually come to low levels and HIV could become a chronic manageable illness in India. But, despite being through three phases till date (NACP-I, II, III), the gravity of the disease has become more prominent and a consensus is yet to be achieved on the effectiveness of the means used and proposed. A social phenomenon invariably depends on societal values, the perception of fear and the menace of the disease to individuals versus perception of the collective. Among major risk groups, this fear influenced by various ideologies and societal goals, is more pronounced than the responses of the society warrant (Velimirovic, 1987 as cited in Temu et al., 2008). NACO documents also describe HIV & AIDS 'as one of the fourteen major communicable diseases that affect the population in India' (NACO, Press Release, 1 December 2006). NACO posters also socially constructed HIV & AIDS as an incurable disease (*laailaaj bimari*). The entire discourse about it revolved around the fact that, it is not the fear and dilemma that restrains people from engaging in certain kinds of sexual behaviour, but motivates them to engage in it with minimum risk. The reluctance of society to address openly issues of sexual behaviour has started diminishing at various levels with the government making efforts to introduce sexual health as a subject at school level. There is rapidly accumulating knowledge on the social influence in the spread of the disease, but as yet, scant information on the influence of social factors on the control efforts and effectiveness of preventive behavioural strategies. Social, cultural norms, beliefs and values are the societal drivers of HIV, as evidenced by social and political sciences. It has also got highlighted in the political context of institutions and networks that shape the epidemic and response. Thus, HIV & AIDS becomes a 'social' disease that needs to be analysed both on biomedical and environmental factors.

The resolution adopted by the United General Assembly on HIV & AIDS (UNAIDS, 2001: 25):

> [R]ecognises that poverty, underdevelopment and illiteracy are among the principal contributing factors to the spread of HIV & AIDS and notes with grave concern that HIV & AIDS is compounding poverty and is now reversing or impeding the development in many countries.

The debate over the various structural determinants and their influence upon an individual's capacity to respond is a matter of fact, but to holistically understand the 'social impacts of the pandemic'; the economic and structural drivers have to be carefully studied. This will help us to understand how people live their lives in daily context, become infected, and respond to HIV & AIDS. Most of the communication campaigns in the epidemic model have not attempted to look at HIV & AIDS as an entirely medical problem but also as a social problem that affects the society at large. HIV & AIDS eventually got constructed as a social disease, and this study attempts to understand how communication campaigns have been designed. The persons living with HIV & AIDS have to learn how to be victims of a social disease and how to represent themselves as such. HIV & AIDS is a major cause for worry for the policymakers and communication planners, which the resolution adopted by the United General Assembly on declaration on HIV & AIDS (2001) accepts:

> [T]hat all people, rich and poor, without distinction as to age, gender or race, are affected by the HIV & AIDS epidemic. It further notes people in developing countries are the most affected and that woman, young adults and children are the most vulnerable (point 4).

The general notion that guided the entire HIV & AIDS campaign in India was that it principally affects the poor. HIV & AIDS is a complex disease, medically. It is a disease for which there is no known cure—and for which existing treatments are economically and organisationally beyond the reach of most of those who suffer from it. As a social disease it reflects social conditions: the fragility of rural economies and the lack of social power of persons affected with HIV & AIDS. The high prevalence rate of HIV & AIDS among the poor reflects the high levels of migration of men, impelled by the crisis of agriculture and rural development. The earliest of the HIV & AIDS campaigns emphasised this factor, where upon it was suggested that migrants who go in search for work to cities, solicit casual/paid sex with prostitutes (later called Commercial Sex Workers or CSW) and bring the 'virus' back home to their spouses. Even truck drivers/helpers, who were also targeted by the HIV & AIDS campaign were considered prone to solicit sex on the highway.

> The Healthy Highways project in India in the mid-1990s was designed to reach long-distance truck drivers with safer sex messages at truck stops, where intercourses with commercial sex workers often take place. This HIV prevention intervention failed until formative research showed the public health professionals how to think like a lower-class truck driver.
> (Rogers, 2003:86)

The Healthy Highways Project was developed by the Social Marketing and Communication Unit (SOMAC) of Lowe-Lintas advertisement agency. This project was funded by NACO, the British Commission Health and Population office and the Department of International Development (DFID). An entire range of behaviour change materials were developed for the project, which was implemented by over 35 NGOs across the country working directly with the target groups i.e., truckers, their assistants, their sexual partners and families, employers and sex workers. Interpersonal, stand-alone and take-away media materials included: flip charts, mobile photo exhibitions, posters, condom fliers, audio tapes, booklets, etc. Story-based communication was being used in all appropriate media. The role model (*Ustaad*) was created to address messages to all truck drivers. He was likeable, macho and funny and spoke to the target group as a friend/elder brother, giving them tips and advising them on behaviour through his own examples. His loyal helper (*Vijay*) was young and mischievous and looked up to *Ustaad* for guidance. These types of campaigns reflect the spread of prostitution as a means of survival. Inferences were also drawn on the fact that poor women in rural society have the least social power to control their own sexuality and consequences arising out of it. There have been instances where the poor had to sell off all their belongings to pay for the health facilities. Possessions thus sold came in handy to compensate for the 'man-days' lost by the infected person. Such kind of association of HIV & AIDS with poverty has a very devastating effect on the economy as well as the sociological thinking in the society. An early death of the bread winner (truckers and migrant workers in this case) leaves an indelible mark on the entire family. As a result of which the young children (orphan and vulnerable children) are forced to take to work in order to fend for their family. If it is a male child, then he will definitely find some work, but being a girl child and to work—sometimes leads them to sex work. Therefore, the entire cycle of vulnerability and poverty continues. One such poster developed by Family Health International (FHI) and NACO highlighted the concept of decision-making in a woman in such a vulnerable situation. In the poster the 'body' of a female has been divided into four parts. The top or the head portion discusses about a women's right to take decisions regarding her sexual health and preferences. The second portion (bust) is about right of control over her body (*sharir par apna hak*). The third portion depicts the abdomen portion, which indicates her preference to save her child from HIV infection, and the final part depicts her remaining part of the body, where she asserts her right for safe sex (*surakshit sammbhog*). Looking at this poster, it can be inferred that a woman's body parts are shown in accordance to the function that they have to perform to adhere to a societal norm. This poster constructs the body of a woman in terms of its functionalities. The third and the fourth part indicate functionality of a woman in terms of motherhood and as a sexual partner. This poster can also be understood in the perspective of how various structural determinants have a larger influence on the epidemic called HIV & AIDS, where the medical realm is relegated to the background and issues like decision-making, right of choice and right to safe sex come into discussion. This is where the campaign takes it to the other level where involvement of the women in change (*parivartan*) cannot be ruled out. Thereby, strengthening the argument and constructing HIV & AIDS as a social disease.

## Moralistic model

With the end of the Cold War, Western donors set the democratisation of politics, good governance and prudent management of the economy as standards for continued donor assistance to developing countries (Tumushabe,

2006). Around 2002, ABCD (Abstinence, Behaviour Change, Condom and Drugs) emerged as a dominant theme to represent the approaches that worked best in reducing the prevalence of HIV. In reality, only pre-marital abstinence was promoted, since advocating for marital fidelity was more difficult in the patriarchal system that characterises India. The proponents of ABCD have not provided convincing evidence as to which of the three assumed factors—abstinence, being faithful to one's partner or condom use—is responsible for the different levels of prevalence among different population subgroups. As with the trend world over, the condom was presented as the only way or the best way to protect against the spread of virus. This unipolar focus on the condom has also led to the barrier in accepting the messages as well as association with the subject of sex. Though there is no denying the fact that the condom is a useful and appropriate prevention method for some, its propagation as a universal prevention method has also undermined the other prevention options i.e., abstinence and fidelity (NACO, 2004).

### The ABCD approach and moralisation of HIV & AIDS campaign

The key issues in Behaviour Change Communication relate to getting the combination of Abstinence, Behaviour Change, Condom and Drugs (ABCD) messages through different channels. The impressive rise in the levels of awareness about HIV & AIDS in the general community can be partly attributed to the electronic media that has taken this message right up to the village level. The Government of India took notice of this and wanted to reinforce positive cultural and social values like love, warmth and affection within the family through its campaigns. Avoidance of multi-partner sexual relationships, use of condoms and sexual abstinence are usually advocated for prevention of spread of HIV and other sexually transmitted diseases. One such poster caters to this reinforcement of cultural and social values by the Government of India. The poster points out the *Panchsheel* (Five virtues) of a successful life. They are *Shaadi ke umar mein ho shaadi* (Marriage at the right age)—one of the virtues in the poster asking for abstinence; *Ek hi ho jeevan saathi* (only one life partner/monogamous marriage), *surakshit ho youn sambandh* (safe sexual relationships)—both are indicators of fidelity—are indications to this. *Panchsheel* translated into Sanskrit would mean 'five virtues'. Thus, messages like this attempt to reinstate and reinforce the 'virtues' of a social life back into the Indian society.

### Social construction of abstinence and controlled sexual behaviour

The principal strategy of the *National AIDS Prevention and Control Policy* (NACO, 2002:8) for prevention and control of the disease is in 'Reinforcing the traditional Indian moral values among youth and other impressionable groups of the population'. The primary audience for this approach is adolescents who are not yet sexually active. Religious teachings, family values in

India and the desire for educational advancement and related factors encourage abstinence. The sexual health messages on abstinences are clinically accurate, but moral judgments about self-control and sexuality are deeply embedded in the call for abstinence. The posters did not give a clear indication on age or directions based on which young people should involve in safer sexual activities. At the same time, moral assumptions in the messages may not reflect the cultural practices and beliefs in India.

On the other hand, peer pressure, biological changes etc., may lead to sexual relations before marriage. This approach of the Government of India mainly focused efforts on protecting 'vulnerable' children. Thereby, sexuality gets constructed on moral grounds around the issues of purity, self-restraint and the denial of sexual pleasure in young people (Cheng, 2005). Thus, the health message for young people to abstain from premarital and extramarital sex was very much prominent in the messages of NACO (2004:15), where in it states that: 'abstinence is the only sure way to prevent sexual transmission of AIDS and other sexually transmitted diseases'. NACO came up with posters that made direct reference to the 'right age for sexual debut' wherein the posters clearly stated that the the young should practice abstinence and give more emphasis on studies and sports. Posters also tried to demotivate the youth from indulging in sex at an early age and insisted, 'wait till you attain the right age', but there is no clear indication of what the right age is. Red colour is again predominant in such images to underline the fact, that this is the only way (abstinence) to keep HIV away ('for success pave way and keep HIV & AIDS at bay'), what actually the messages intend to. Yet, most of the sexual transmission that is responsible for the spread of the disease happens after marriage, since many Indian girls are married before they reach the age of 18. And homosexual transmission is often parallel to a traditional couple's lifestyle, where a person could be heterosexual and homosexual at the same time. While the health message in the posters is clinically accurate, the moral judgments by the state about self-control and sexuality are embedded in the call for abstinence. Personal choice over when and how to engage in safer sexual activities is less prominent. And while moral assumptions may not reflect the cultural practices and beliefs of many Indian young people, all HIV & AIDS prevention programmes funded by the international donors were required to promote abstinence. It is not just the content of the abstinence health message, but also who has the power to determine the content of the health messages. There was always a clear indication that the artwork and messages are borrowed from the West while constructing HIV amongst the young. The characters (the colour of the hair, the hairstyles, the dressing pattern) shown in the posters are difficult to relate to the Indian context. Even the punchline, 'Come join our gang and give HIV a bang!'—sounds somewhat like imported lingo. ABC has become little more than an excuse and justification to promote the Indian government's long-standing agenda regarding people's sexual behaviour and the kind of sex education they should receive – A for unmarried people, bolstered by advocacy of B, but for most people, 'anything but C' (Cohen, 2003). However, abstinence is difficult in practice. Virgins are prized by older men attempting to avoid contacting HIV infections (Gupta, 2000). This places young girls at risk for becoming infected by men who may already be HIV positive. Women also suffer from forced sex. The force may be physical such as in rape, but women may also be forced into sex purely for survival. In areas which have been badly hurt by economic recession, many women and girls find economic refuge in 'sexual networking', or exchanging sexual favours for money, gifts and protection (Singhal & Rogers, 2003). Posters also propagated the state's discourse on *sanyam, wafadari and samajhdari* (abstinence, fidelity and intelligence) and emphasises on *AIDS ki bachchne ki tayyari* (to prepare oneself to protect from AIDS). One such poster developed by NACO seemed like a direct acceptance by the government that people do indulge in pre-marital sex (which questions the abstinence approach) and are not faithful to their spouse (which questions the fidelity approach). One of the posters brought out during that period, mentions two steps in order to address the morals to the society about HIV & AIDS. It says; A—abstain from pre-marital sex; B—be faithful to your spouse; C—if A and B is not practised, use condom. In this pattern of abstinence, condoms are often depicted as useless since the two lovers arrived pristine to their marriage and are supposed to remain loyal to each other. The state's conceptualisation of the sexual citizenship of its subjects is interesting. The right of choice (to have sex or not with multiple partners) unambiguously gets constructed as a masculine one. Male desire is constitutive of the state's discourse on AIDS. The primary issue here is about exercising the choice; to remain celibate before marriage and monogamous after is purely a male decision.

### Prescribing faithfulness amongst 'partners'

The National IEC/BCC Strategic Framework for HIV & AIDS Programme (NACO, 2004: 10) suggests that it should base its strategy firmly in the cultural realities of Indian behaviour patterns and belief systems, and address the constraints and limitations facing individuals attempting to initiate new behaviours within existing social structures and personal relationships, such as social norms, perceptions of self-efficacy and power inequalities in male/female relationships. It is not clear how the National AIDS Control Organisation bases its argument about 'Indian behaviour pattern and belief systems'. It tends to posit its argument back to the 'conservative, closed, patriarchal and single partner relationships' that had been guiding all its campaigns. Therefore, to establish and ask for new phenomena such as abstinence and fidelity demand a huge shift in focus. This focus should also be located in the wider domain of 'social norms' and the 'power inequalities in male/female relationships' (NACO, 2004). Few posters were reflective of such strategic shift in communication of sexual messages in the context of pre-conceived notions of family and patriarchy. The target audience in this case are married couples or unmarried but sexually active individuals. The main intention is to reduce the number of partners. In cases where one partner is unfaithful or people are into short-term relationships it's not very effective. Communication addressed the prevalent social norms in this approach—family as a unit where the presence of a child was used to reinforce the family concept. This is a point from which, the state has taken over the dissemination of sexual health into its subjects. During NACP-II most of the communication material focused on this. A key feature of this shift also led to certain problems, where the general impression that 'everyone is doing it' and it is alright to have sex in pre- and post-marital relationships also gained ground largely due to liberal media, easy access to money and the revolution in information technology (NACO, 2002). Having subtly accepted that such relationships do exist, the state, campaigned for HIV testing of either of the partners or both for a 'happy married life'.

### *Repositioning condoms as tool for sexual control*

The target for the condom campaign was the sexually active population that included men and women who could influence the men. The problem faced in this approach is that it was more acceptable to young educated people and to those having sexual relationship outside marriage. One such poster attempted to address the concerns of a 'father' or a bread earner of a family towards his family. It is a bit confusing. Does the poster imply, that the man of the house indulges in sex outside his home, with someone who is a HIV-infected person? Thus, the 'love for my family'! Or does the poster mean he is aware of his 'risky behaviour' and is 'motivated' to use a condom as a fall-out of 'love for his family'. The same can be related to another poster that instructs the man to use a condom to put on leash (*ankush*) HIV & AIDS but not on pleasure (*anand*). The poster also illustrates HIV & AIDS as a *jaanleva bimari* (life-threatening disease), which again constructs it into a social disease in the psyche of the population exposed to such messages. The problems related to intensive use of condom and condomisation of the population has been discussed in Chapter 5.

### *Re-establishment of the injecting drug user's approach*

Most of posters found under this subhead were from the North Eastern part of India. The sentinel studies indicated high incidence of HIV transmission among the youth who are drug users. Role models were used extensively in reaching out to the young people in this type of campaign. Posters also depicted a teacher, who 'talks to the students about drugs'. Similarly, another one depicts a parent who talks to his son about drugs. One such poster shares the concerns of a young woman wanting to get pregnant. The posters accept the fact that the young woman indulged in 'sharing needles' or has had 'unsafe sex' and or has had 'infected blood transfusion' that has 'damaged' her prospects of getting pregnant. Though the message focuses primarily on the modes of transmission i.e., mother to child, it stereotypically constructs the basic function of a woman as that of reproduction. This message is located in the context of an infected person. The main message, 'Prevent STD, HIV & AIDS' in the poster gets relegated to the background.

### Empowering the young through sexual health education

Over half of all new infections worldwide each year are among young people between the ages of 15 and 24. Every day, more than 5,000 young people become infected with HIV—more than five every minute. Yet the needs of the world's over one billion young people are often ignored when strategies on HIV & AIDS are drafted, policies developed and budgets allocated. This is especially tragic as young people are more likely than adults to adopt and maintain safe behaviours. Young people are vulnerable to HIV infection because they lack the crucial information, education and services to protect themselves. Messages were developed to raise the awareness levels of the young people about HIV & AIDS. Poster were developed that described the modes of transmission in the form of 'real life' experience between two young friends, one of whom is HIV infected. In India, young people in the age group 15–24 years comprise almost 25% of the country's population; however, they account for 31% of the AIDS burden (NACO/MOHFW, 2007a). Social interaction with the opposite sex, peer pressure and poverty, are the contributory factors for increased sexual activity and promiscuity amongst the young people (Kirby, 2002; Romer et al., 1994). In a conservative society like India, where sex-related issues constitute a taboo for discussion, young people are hindered from actively seeking counselling regarding sexual health. Young people often carry negative connotation in their mind because of social ostracism and HIV & AIDS-associated stigma (Nath, 2009). This results in lack of knowledge about self-protection measures, leading to a silent spread of the disease. Despite these worrisome statistics, some Indian states have banned sex education in schools, following protests from legislators that it would have a negative impact on the vulnerable minds of school students. Widespread ignorance about the disease is still prevalent, even among youth belonging to the affluent sections of society. This emerging epidemic in the young, who comprise the most productive age group, will certainly have an adverse impact on the country's economy.

Communication has been described as a 'social vaccine' (UNAIDS, 2001), and it can serve as a powerful preventive tool. Initiatives to spread awareness among the youth are being vigorously undertaken by the government, private and non-governmental organisations. In spite of all this, there is still a gap between the amount invested in developing a curriculum and the actual education that is imparted. Until now, most of the HIV & AIDS education has been 'scientific in nature', i.e. discussed in the biological context by teachers of science. However, for AIDS education to have a realistic impact, it is important that instruction be imparted in a straightforward, easy to grasp manner, keeping cultural issues in mind. In a spearheading effort, the NACO collaborated with UNICEF to scale up the school-based adolescence programme across government schools, with the objective of reaching out to students. Despite the challenge posed by the HIV & AIDS epidemic, sex education programmes have been banned in six states in India, including Maharashtra, Gujarat, Rajasthan, Madhya Pradesh, Chattisgarh and Karnataka (Voice of America, 2007, as cited in Nath, 2009).

### Religion and HIV & AIDS: Moralising population

HIV & AIDS as an epidemic has been addressed by the Faith-Based Organisations (FBOs) in many countries. Though, the National AIDS Control Society has tried to do something by involving Muslim clerics to spread awareness about HIV & AIDS in the Muslim population, it has not tried to do anything similar with other religious communities in India. The majority of India's Hindu population have not been reached through any religious discourses anywhere. India has many religious leaders with huge followers, but none of them has ever deliberated on HIV & AIDS. During the early years of the HIV & AIDS epidemic, many people who worked in HIV & AIDS prevention thought of religious leaders and organisations as naturally antagonistic to what they were trying to accomplish. In many minds, the stereotype of a religious leader was that of a conservative moralist who disapproved of any form of sexual behaviour outside of marriage as well as what was seen as the 'only solution' to HIV infection, i.e., condoms. An important point that policymakers remembered when taking action is that there are many organisations and individuals who respond to HIV & AIDS and who want to be of service. Thus, it was felt by the Government of India that religious leaders and Faith-Based Organisations have enormous influence on people's attitudes and value systems. In order to mobilise their support, NACO initiated an Indian interfaith council for HIV & AIDS activities. In many cases, this would mean providing the compassion and moral support that can break through the judgment, shame and fear so often associated with HIV & AIDS. Religious leaders can also foster the process of reconciliation that is so urgently needed to bring families and communities divided by HIV & AIDS back together. The principles of compassion, leadership and moral responsibility that people of all faiths embrace was felt to be urgently needed to halt the spread of HIV and alleviate the suffering caused by AIDS. Religious leaders and those associated with Faith-Based Organisations as trusted and respected members of society, are able to get the attention of their respective communities (*My Voice Matters,* another phase of campaign undertaken by NACO to promote AIDS awareness among various religious and ethnic groups). Their actions were thought to set an example. This can be especially instrumental in eradicating the stigma and discrimination against people living with HIV & AIDS. Morals were ingrained into the masses where the religious leaders drew examples from their own religion about abstinence (*brahma charya* in case of Hinduism) etc. Metaphors like evil, sin and death were also invoked during such deliberations by the religious leaders.

## Economic/organisational model

### Economics and the world of work

HIV & AIDS is a major threat to the world of work. It has shown maximum impact on the most productive segment of the labour force. In countries with high HIV prevalence rates, it has cut the supply of labour and slashed the incomes of workers, adversely affected enterprise performance and national economies. The Government of India's National Policy on HIV & AIDS and the World of Work (NACO, 2009:4) states:

> HIV & AIDS also affects fundamental rights at work, particularly with respect to discrimination and stigmatization of workers and people living with and affected by HIV & AIDS. Stigma and discrimination at the workplace gets reflected in the form of loss of employment and livelihood opportunities in addition to ostracism and seclusion faced by workers either due to known or presumed HIV status.

The National Policy on HIV & AIDS and the World of Work (2009) was formulated by the Ministry of Labour and Employment while ratifying the ILO Convention No. 111 on Discrimination (Employment and Occupation). This policy statement was formulated for non-discrimination amongst workers on the basis of their real or perceived HIV status. The increased mortality results in a smaller skilled population and labour force. The labour force in India predominantly consists of young people. A sick family member or a time off on sickness lowers the productivity levels. Increased mortality due to HIV & AIDS also has an impact on the available family resources that could be through loss of income or by death of any or both of the parents. AIDS also seriously reduces available resources for public expenditures such as education and health services not related to AIDS. This results in increase in pressure for the state's finances and slower growth of the economy. Policy-makers world over do understand the burden that HIV & AIDS imposes on its economies. Appropriate measures need to be ensured that there are adequate public resources in the future in order to prevent or mitigate the human catastrophe that the epidemic threatens to unleash (Greener, 2002). AIDS results in both the loss of income and increased spending on healthcare by a household. However, HIV & AIDS patients will have to worry less about getting enough food and shelter and more about fighting their disease.

Campaigns in the economic model specifically centred around the discourse on the concepts of 'productive age group' and the 'economic loss'. Posters were funded specifically by the International Labour Organization (ILO). A closer look at the posters would reveal that most of the working class that is shown came from the unorganised sector. It does not show any from the organised corporate sector. An assumption can be made here is that most of the artwork that was used in India was borrowed from the West, and the images as well as messages were built on their perceptions. Though later on, messages were developed were more Indian, that showed Indian working conditions. AIDS was still shown in red colour, leading to further discrimination amongst the labour force. Against this background, one of the posters focused on 'softening the blow' on economy due to 'HIV & AIDS hits hardest at people in the 15–49 age group'. India has a working population of over 400 million, 93% of whom are in the informal economy. The informal/ unorganised sector labour is hard to reach and is characterised by low literacy, negligible social protection benefits, difficult working conditions, poor health-seeking behaviour and limited access to health services (National Policy on HIV & AIDS and the World of Work, 2009). A large number of people migrate, both internally as well as overseas in search of better employment/livelihood opportunities. Though not all migrant workers are at equal risk, the process of migration enhances vulnerability to infections such as HIV, particularly to those who are single, stay away from families for long durations and work under difficult conditions. Images outlined the ILO codes of practice on HIV & AIDS. The principles insist on the various aspects of recognising HIV & AIDS as a workplace issue. Contrasting images were also there in their message content and are emotionally loaded. These messages insist on social dialogues amongst workers regarding HIV & AIDS and urge non-discrimination and no HIV & AIDS screening of its workers from the employers. NACO's poster showed a group of tailors in a small garment manufacturing unit, where the employer does not 'discriminate' his/her workers on the basis of their 'HIV status', whereas in another poster a person who was fired from his job because of his HIV status was shown. HIV & AIDS unquestionably has an economic impact. AIDS causes the death of young and able-bodied people in the most productive part of their life. Thus, it was expected that AIDS would have a powerful negative economic impact. In the initial years of the HIV & AIDS epidemic, it was widely believed that the epidemic would have a catastrophic impact on economies of all countries, especially those of developing countries.

## Political model

The political model of social construction of HIV & AIDS in India is basically centred around the concept of the state. The state here is the guiding institutional authority with regards to HIV & AIDS programmes and policies. The HIV & AIDS epidemic has definitely elicited the state's concern about the inequalities in health service delivery amongst its population. It is also equally aware about the unequal impact of the epidemic. Unreported cases or people not coming forward to report about their HIV status and being silent about it, was also a major concern for it. In such a scenario, the Government of India attempted to construct this phenomenon as a major health problem and aimed to seek the larger participation and involvement of the population at large. The political model is centred on the construction of collective action by the people as well as the state. The HIV & AIDS messages were focussed on the metaphors of 'responsibility', 'promise' and 'accountability'. Thereby, the messages that were disseminated suggested that each and every individual, as a citizen, has a collective responsibility to fight the epidemic.

### *HIV & AIDS and the construction of war and victory*

This section explores the discourse of war against HIV & AIDS evident in the campaign messages and discusses the implications of this approach in terms of how HIV & AIDS gets constructed. This framework depends fundamentally on the prominence that is accorded to HIV & AIDS, and which allows for its construction as the enemy. The government in this context takes on the role of a commander, directing the war through policy and intervention strategies. Ordinary citizens are incited to take on prevention and caring roles.

Posters talked about *bharat ke pratinidhi* (ambassadors of India) and their collective role against AIDS *ke khilaaf ladney* (the fight against AIDS) and *dayitv nibhane* (fulfilling responsibility). The terms *pratinidhi, ladney* and *dayitv* drive home the inherent duties that a citizen has to fulfil towards the state. HIV & AIDS thus constructs the framework of a responsible citizen who indulges in responsible sexual behaviour and becomes a partner in the 'fight' against AIDS. Thus, fulfils her/his duties toward the state. Images also drives deep the message of 'promise'—to stop AIDS. The thumb impression is to signify the illiterate masses that are to be reached and should become part and parcel of this entire 'promise to stop AIDS'. In a micro process, HIV & AIDS can also be described as something similar to cancer—as an invasion. It is seen as infiltrating a society, sometimes hiding for years (Sontag, 1991). However, when focus shifts to transmission of the disease, a different and older metaphor is invoked, that of pollution (Connelly & Macleod, 2003). HIV & AIDS is transmitted by blood or sexual fluid of infected people or from contaminated blood products. This allows for the construction of what Sacks (1996:69) calls the 'diseased body', the polluter, the transmitter of disease, the infector.

The deployment of a war discourse with regard to HIV & AIDS invokes certain practices, feelings and (e.g. aggressive technological strategies as opposed to, say, the development of coping), particular feelings (fear, dependence on the part of 'patients'; power, responsibility on the part of health practitioners) and power relations. It potentially deepens existing forms of oppression, while suppressing alternative ways of understanding HIV & AIDS.

(Connelly & Macleod, 2003:3)

Images also socially constructed the 'resolve' of the nation to 'fight AIDS' and *vijay ki tayyari* (preparing for victory). The discourse of HIV & AIDS as 'war' constructs at least four categories of subjects who are positioned in relations of power. First is HIV & AIDS as the enemy along with the 'diseased body' as an infector. Then there are commanders/leaders who direct the battle and the social construction of control, after which are experts who are bolstered by the powerful discourse of (Western) science and medicine and lastly, the members of the society who are affected by the war as victims or people at risk (Connelly & Macleod, 2003). A war discourse reinforces the institution of government that is central to leading the nation and funding the war effort. Government leaders and other political players gain from the construction of war against HIV & AIDS through involvement in planning and strategy. The discursive framework of war implies greater strategy and planning that is necessary. The weapon of choice in the war against HIV & AIDS between 1985 and 2000 was predominantly public education about it. Though, in 1986, this took the form of scientific information from experts, from 1990 there was a greater focus on prevention and education campaigns supplemented by scientific information. Potential use of drugs in order to prevent infection and control of its effects became a prominent form of discourse since 2000. The deployment of war discourse has a silencing effect. In particular, it is people affected by HIV & AIDS whose voices are silenced. A campaign in support of and focusing on the People Living with HIV & AIDS was undertaken. Separate efforts and policies were formulated to bring this section of the population into the mainstream.

# 5 Social construction of masculinity
## Condomisation of sexual health

The condom is widely used as a barrier device by males around the world. In India, it is known by its trade name *Nirodh*, a Sanskrit word meaning 'prevention'. Condom has been used extensively as an effective simple 'spacing' method of contraception, without side effects. In addition, condoms are used to prevent pregnancies and protect both men and women from sexually transmitted diseases. The Ministry of Health and Family Welfare (MoHFW) has been promoting condoms as an option for contraception in India since the late 1960s and has been responsible for the generic promotion, condom procurement and supply. This contributed significantly to increased condom use in northern states like Uttar Pradesh and Punjab. However, condom use was low in South Indian states where female sterilisation was the main focus of family planning programme. (NACO, 2011:8). National AIDS Control Organisation (NACO) has launched a number of innovative approaches in promotion of condom use. Condom Vending Machines (CVM) were established by NACO. The CVMs, numbering around 11,025, offered access to quality condoms at any time, in a non-embarrassing manner[1]. Another 11,025 CVMs were installed in all the metros and major cities across the country during NACP-II. A pre-programming assessment for social marketing of female condoms was undertaken to implement Female Condoms (FC) in select locations of eight states. This was done to understand the acceptability, willingness to pay, and its impact on dual protection. Ministry of Health and Family Welfare funded the procurement of 500,000 FC to be promoted amongst female sex workers in six states and among general population in two states. Apart from these measures, thicker, more lubricated condoms branded as 'Spice Up' was launched in collaboration with Hindustan Latex Family Planning Promotion Trust (HLFPPT) to cater to special needs of the high-risk groups. These condoms were again socially marketed in the targeted intervention sites. Men did not bother to use condoms when one of the partners is sterilised or using an intra-uterine devices (IUDs) for birth control. Basically, condom use is a male-controlled method. The first nationwide contraceptive social marketing programme, the *Nirodh* condom project in India, began in 1967 with funding from the Ford Foundation. The substantial increase in condom sales was attributed to the distribution and promotion of condoms at a subsidised price. The government adopted a conscious policy of promoting use of condoms through the social marketing and community-based distribution system (National AIDS Control and Prevention Policy, 2003). The success of the Indian experience informed subsequent social marketing interventions such as the distribution of infant-weaning formula in public health clinics. Promotion of condoms through social marketing had its own drawbacks. The reluctance of people to tailor behaviour to the recommendations of social marketing campaigns, and the fact that campaigns need to be adjusted to socio-cultural contexts and morals are evidence that social marketing lacks the much-attributed power of manipulating audiences. Social marketing's conception of participation basically constructs the campaigns' targets as 'passive receivers', subjects from whom information is obtained to change products and concepts. The National AIDS Control Programme (NACP) has been promoting condom use as a safe sex practice for prevention of STI/RTI and HIV and protection from unwanted pregnancy, which ultimately led to the Condomisation of the entire country. As was observed in various messages, the communication campaign built into the concept of masculine, where the 'power' and the 'control' are in the hands of a man. NACP-I introduced the targeted intervention, a strategy that eventually became the mainstay of the AIDS programme. Pilot projects were started on the 'targeted interventions' for education and condom promotion amongst groups identified to have high-risk behaviour. As part of its focus on prevention, the government supported the installation of over 11,000 condom vending machines in colleges, roadside restaurants, stations, gas stations and hospitals.

Condom provision, social marketing and focused promotion to different segments particularly high-risk population became the centre-pieces of the AIDS response everywhere in the world (UNAIDS, 2006). India followed suit. There was a lot of criticism of the condom-centric approach of the state and on its attempts at the Condomisation of the entire epidemic. Condom-centric ways or preventing sexually transmitted diseases (STDs), along with Targeted Interventions among High Risk Groups (TIHRG), was advocated with a lot of zeal by the NACO, terming it as cost-effective and was dubbed as the only available preventive method (Chhabra, 2007). Images socially constructed a kind of understanding that it is only the condom that could protect a person from an STD as well as HIV & AIDS. Messages were circulated that depicted the image of a man and urged his 'masculinity' with a condom in the backdrop and urges him to get 'it' on before he gets it 'on'.

Messages related to condom promotion built further into the concepts of masculinity and attempts to tinker with the ego of a man. *Condom ke saath hi asli mardangi ka mazza* (real pleasure of masculinity) plays into the psyche of man and masculinity. Images depicting a semi-nude woman, with a tag, 'No entry without condom', signified the need or desire of a man but with conditions attached. Red colour was used prominently in depicting the 'condom'-word in almost all the messages on condom promotion. Condoms were marketed and promoted as devices of pleasure by the private condom manu-facturing companies, who over a period of time became the key players in the condom market. The pricing mechanism was also competitive. The private players introduced various subvariants in condoms such as lubricated, extra ribbed, ribbed dotted etc. Therefore, these condom manufacturing companies broke the 'traditional' simple *rubber* kind of perceptions amongst the popu-lation and positioned themselves as pleasure devices. These types of condoms were available at the local chemist shops but were not available at the free condom vending machines of the government. The offices of the Hindustan Latex Limited, which was manufacturing the *'moods'* brand of condoms, had a vending machine outside its office, but they were priced. Condoms also started getting sold as brands instead of simply *Nirodh,* which was a generic name. These products were way above the usual *'rubber'* or *'umbrella'* that the government provided at the health centres. The widespread messages on con-doms, created a perception amongst the upwardly mobile and the urban youth that people should just go and ask for brands, if they feel shy to ask for simply condoms. *'Moods please',* or *'Ask for KS'* (Kama Sutra—another brand of condom) were such examples. These private brands promoted the images of pleasure and enjoyment and they comfortably positioned them-selves as 'pregnancy prevention and pleasure deriving device rather than HIV & AIDS prevention device'. These brands also provided customers with explicit details about sexual acts and positions that were derived from the *Kamasutra* (The *Kamasutra* is an ancient Indian Hindu text written by Vāt-syāyana. It is widely considered to be the standard work on human sexual behaviour in Sanskrit literature). This was provided on the inside of the condom packets & leaflets. The (in) famous promotional ads of Kama Sutra are still signified as excellent product positioning strategies by marketing gurus. The Condomisation of HIV & AIDS perhaps for the first time tacitly accepted the reality of sex outside marriage. The communication strategy of the Government of India, therefore, re-engineered its appeal and focused on humour and pleasure. The aggressive Kama Sutra condom campaign with its seductive visual imagery spoke to the young male about undiminished plea-sure with the condom. Its advertising slogan 'dotted for extra pleasure' attempted to break the male perception of condoms as 'un-pleasurable' family planning devices. While the successful Kama Sutra campaign strategy with its new positioning statement increased condom sales, it did not impact the incidence of HIV & AIDS. The most successful and practical way adopted world over to prevent the transmission of HIV was the use of condoms. While the use of condom may seem easy, by formulating a programme to cover the whole country needed careful planning on certain issues. These issues are mainly related to the question that how to sensitise people for using condoms not only for the sake of family planning but also as the best preventive step against HIV and STD. At the same time, it is also very important for the commercial sex workers to convince their clients about the importance of use of condoms as a means for preventing the HIV transmission. The challenges was to make available low cost and good quality condoms to the people all over the country easily at the time and place when they need it (UNODC, 2006: 85–86).

Condoms became a use-and-throw commodity for sexual encounter for the young people. They preferred condoms rather than get embarrassed about getting caught with contraceptive pills. Thus, condom got repositioned again in the context of HIV & AIDS as a tool for pleasure. An interesting fact that emerges here is that the government was trying hard to promote condoms as a protective device for the people against Sexually Transmitted Infections and to protect them from HIV ultimately. It was, at the same time, also was trying to address issues of fidelity, single-partner sex and of faithful companionship through its campaigns on condom promotion. Ironically, private condom manufacturing companies were promoting the condom as a device for uninterrupted, long-lasting pleasures. Condoms got promoted by them as a contraceptive tool, one that prevents unwanted pregnancy. Nowhere did these companies disseminate messages on responsible sexual behaviour nor were they bothered about how to protect oneself from Sexually Transmitted Diseases. They were more concerned about sales. This type of extensive Condomisation approach was criticised for their 'regular partner' approach (Chhabra, 2007). When people live in poor conditions without proper access to health infrastructure, a demand for 'abstinence' may not happen, 'Be faithful' may also not happen, and 'condomise'—people are ready to use them—but have no access to money. Condoms at the same time are not freely available, and at a price that are luxuries many cannot afford. The UN Office for the Coordination of Humanitarian Affairs, 2005 as cited in Kvasny & Chong, (2008) states that 'people can spend that money on either condoms or food … they are not going to spend their food money on a piece of rubber'. Former Ugandan President, Yoweri Musevani, in 1991 had also expressed his reservation about the effectiveness of the condom:

> Just as we were offered the 'magic bullet' in the early 1940s, we are now being offered the condom for 'safe sex'. I feel that condoms have a role to play as a means of protection, especially in couples who are HIV-positive, but they cannot become the main means of stemming the tide of AIDS.
>
> (Green, 2001)

The HIV & AIDS messages that were brought out by the NACO, both in Hindi and English do emphasise about the concept of 'partner' (*Saathi*). Nowhere in the messages, does it talk about 'partner' being a spouse. Another message that was borrowed from a popular pressure cooker advertisement that used to be telecast on TV in the mid-80s, with the same message—*Jo biwi se kartey hain pyar, woh prestige se kaise karein inkaar* (Those who love their wife, how would they refuse prestige pressure cooker). When the same message was carried onto an HIV & AIDS poster, the message does not mention the woman in the poster as wife which is more relevant in the Indian context, but terms her as a 'partner. In a sense, it can mean the 'partner' could be anyone, with whom the man indulges as sexual partner in a risky condition.

One of the main reasons for the failure of the campaigns to promote condom use has been the 'image' of the condom itself. For close to three decades, the condom was popularised as a contraceptive device for family planning. When the focus of the family planning shifted from restricting the number of children to spacing them, it became an ideal spacing device. The HIV crisis from the 1980s onwards positioned the condom as a protective device. Since then, the entire thrust of the communication campaigns, be it social marketing or behaviour change, has solely centred on promoting the idea of 'safe sex'. By replacing the clinical 'clean' sex approach by an upfront, bold, and open approach depicting 'a safer sex that feels good', the condom has now become a key accessory just like a nice perfume or a mobile phone. This type of technique seems to fit the Indian urban well-educated youth who were bored by the biological diagrams, the medical vocabulary and the dried-up explanations. Attempts were also made to popularise the female condom amongst sex workers as well as the general female population, but how far they have been effective is yet to be studied. Posters were developed on female condoms by various AIDS Control societies. The prominent one was by the Mumbai District AIDS Control Society (MDACS). Mumbai being the commercial hub of the country attracts migrant population, who get employed in the organised and unorganised sector. As they stay away from families for a long duration of time, they frequent the red-light area regularly. So, when these people go back home, the chances of spread of HIV & AIDS increases manifold. Thus, a sustained campaign was started in Mumbai by the MDACS to make the commercial sex workers residing in the red-light area more aware about the female condom.

Social marketing is the marketing's sector's way of being 'socially relevant' and 'socially responsible'. The social marketing model centres on communication campaigns designed to promote socially beneficial practices or products in a target group. Marketing strategies such as branding, advertisements, increasing supply outlets to increase condom use is the prime goal. But, quite often this strategy involves subsidies to vendors at all levels, especially to sellers at small shops/outreach workers supplying condoms. They were given low-priced condoms and were allowed to sell at higher prices, keeping a share of the profit for themselves! Social marketing strives to put into practice the well-established standard techniques in the commercial marketing to promote a pro-social behaviour. Social marketing attempts to bring focus on using marketing techniques such as market segmentation and formative research to maximise the effectiveness of interventions and ultimately sales of the 'socially beneficial good—the condom. Though, social marketing motivates young couples to make an informed choice, it fails to address the cultural beliefs that account for risk behaviour or for why people were unwilling to engage in certain health practices even when they are informed about their positive results. This is where HIV & AIDS was addressing the issues of 'deviant' behaviour such as MSM, transgenders, etc. This knowledge went on to become the baseline that allows a successful positioning of a product. This condom got positioned both by the government as well as the private manufacturing companies, in the context of community beliefs. In the next section are the case studies that have been analysed to further elaborate on the Condomisation of the Indian masses.

## Case studies

### Bindaas Bol *and the BBC-World Service Trust Campaign*

With support from the United States Agency for International Development (USAID), the government initiated a campaign called '*Condom Bindaas Bol!*' (Condom—Just say so!), which involved advertising, public events and celebrity endorsements. It aimed to break the taboo that surrounds condom use in India, and to persuade people that they should not be embarrassed to buy them. *Bindaas Bol* campaigns featured Palash Sen (singer), Rohit Roy (TV actor) and Shekar Suman (TV/film actor). This type of campaign was innovative in approach, where the government was promoting and making the condom a 'taboo free' device. Some more films also came up later, that involved railway porters, a group of lawyers, etc.

In 2002, the BBC World Service Trust, NACO, Doordarshan and All India Radio, with the support of DFID, launched a campaign aimed at increasing the awareness of HIV & AIDS in India (Sood, et. al., 2006). The media campaign was aimed at preventing the spread of HIV & AIDS in the north Indian states. In a country where discussing sexual health is still considered taboo, using TV and radio to promote changes in behaviour and attitudes towards HIV & AIDS has proved an effective way of tackling the problem. The campaign developed new programme strands to reinforce key messages about HIV & AIDS. These were primarily aimed at young people to protect themselves and for an end to discrimination against those living with AIDS. The programme included:

- An interactive detective drama, entitled *Jasoos Vijay* broadcast three times a week on Doordarshan;
- A weekly 'reality' show called *Haath se Haath Mila;*
- 'Chat Chowk', a weekly radio phone in programme on personal health issues;
- Advertising spots broadcast three times daily on both TV and radio for the duration of the programme.

One such campaign undertaken during this initiative, is about a character called *Chunnilal*, who in spite of being a forgetful person, never forgets a condom. A total of 1,000 individual broadcasts were aimed to reach more than half the Indian population. More than 3,500 video screenings were made in villages with limited access to TV. A survey was taken out by Nielson to understand the impact of the campaign, of which the most interesting part of a survey was that the TV spots were reaching 43 million people at the cost of less than a rupee and was able to change changing behaviour for less than Rs. 10 per person.

### Balbir Pasha campaign

Population Services International (PSI) executed an aggressive, innovative communication campaign in Mumbai, as part of an integrated behaviour change HIV & AIDS prevention programme called 'Operation Lighthouse'. The project was implemented in 12 major port communities across India with the financial support of the USAID through the AIDS-Mark funding mechanism. This campaign was created by Social Marketing and Communications Unit (SOMAC) of Lowe Worldwide (Lintas earlier). The campaign was based on consumer research analysis and that suggested that HIV infection rates coupled with flawed risk perception as the prominent reason for the prevalence of HIV & AIDS in the poorest sectors of Mumbai. Most of the characters that were depicted on the ads, short films and teasers were basically people living in the Mumbai. Through a mixture of strategically placed outdoor communications, television and radio messages. The was comprehensively covered through newspapers.

The character 'Balbir Pasha'—a fictitious character portrayed various intriguing scenarios, served as a behavioural model for consumers of Mumbai mass media. The theoretical framework that guided this campaign was Albert Bandura's social learning theory (1986), where people learn and change by observing the behaviours of others—risk behaviours in this case. For example, a short film is about a fictitious character called Hariya, who is a migrant labourer working in Mumbai and solicits commercial sex occasionally. What the films insisted on is whether Hariya uses a condom while engaging in such 'risk behaviour'. Another short film is about a character, Manu, who is a 22-year-old 'smart' young man. He is into a relationship with another girl, and the underlying message in it is that because they know each other well, the use of condom is not so necessary. The film later on goes on to say the girl with whom Manu is involved has many other explicit relationships with other men. Later on, many other short films also dwell on the theory of 'regular partner' and of no necessity of condom with them. The Balbir Pasha campaign drew a lot of criticism for socially constructing the woman as the 'carrier' of the virus, where men have to save themselves from such vectors, by using condoms.

One of the most celebrated achievements of the campaign is the way in which the 'Balbir Pasha' icon became entrenched in popular culture. The concept was borrowed by numerous groups and individuals and used the campaign in a different context. In Andhra Pradesh, the character was known as '*Puli Raju* (Tiger King)'. Even Amul, one of the nation's leading dairy co-operatives, borrowed the concept of 'regular partner' when advertising their butter. The theme of 'alcohol and condom use' was more readily accepted but the campaign faced criticism when the theme of 'regular partners' was introduced. Probably for the first time, many individuals openly criticised the Balbir Pasha campaign for its cutting-edge frankness. No other HIV & AIDS campaign brought the deliberations of the bedroom into the living room. This criticism was more specifically aimed at the television commercials that were produced as part of the 'Balbir Pasha' campaign, rather than the outdoor billboards and posters and other communication media. The campaign was also perceived as 'anti-women' as it depicted the male character (Balbir Pasha) as at risk of contracting HIV & AIDS since he is having unprotected sex with a woman (Manjula), thereby implying that HIV is passed on from the woman to the man and she is the carrier of the virus. In addition to the fact that women named Manjula took personal offense (and called the *Saadhan* helpline to express their outrage), some women's groups made a point to argue that the name Manjula targeted a specific religious group.

Still others felt that the campaign was not 'complete' as they felt it only focused on the (hetero) sexual mode of transmission of HIV & AIDS. However, pre-campaign evaluations specifically designed to test for comprehension demonstrated that test subjects could easily understand the campaign's intended messages. It made people sit up and take note of AIDS. It spoke to people in a language they understood. This campaign implied that Westernised campaign may not work to spread awareness among the masses as was done by the National AIDS Control Society in the NACP-I phase. Women's groups called the campaign sexist because it implied that HIV was spread primarily from women to men. But this was because the campaign was targeted at men who frequented CSWs. PSI India chose the group at highest risk, in this case urban men, because it believed that men can play a much stronger role in reducing the epidemic and that no single campaign can successfully address all groups. This campaign followed the principle based upon the UNAIDS approach of 'men make a difference', which places greater responsibility on men to change attitudes and behaviour, which in turn would enable the empowerment of women necessary for protection from HIV infection.

### '*What Kind of Man Are You?*' campaign

Breakthrough, an international human rights organisation launched the 360-degree media campaign, 'What Kind of Man Are You?'. The press brief of Breakthrough (2005) campaign states 'What Kind of Man Are You?' is the first mass-media campaign in India that directly asked the men to wear condoms to protect their wives from HIV & AIDS infection. It put a spotlight on the fact that more than two million married women with

HIV & AIDS in India are infected by their husbands. A taboo issue within Indian society, the campaign questioned stereotypes and created national dialogue about a woman's right to negotiate safe sex within her marriage. The campaign was created by the advertising agency McCann Erickson. The primary focus of creating such a campaign on women and HIV & AIDS was a real challenge and it attempted to understand what a woman would say to her husband in a complex situation like HIV & AIDS. This campaign also encouraged married couples to get involved in dialogue on gender relations and HIV & AIDS. It also attempted to address the issue through text-message-based HIV & AIDS helpline with a popular portal. It claims that this sort of helpline received more than 10,000 queries. 'What Kind of Man Are You?' was stated as a 360-degree integrated communications campaign (TV, radio, print, internet, movie theatres and transportation) that encouraged dialogue on HIV & AIDS among married couples in seven languages: Bengali, Hindi, English, Kannada, Tamil, Telugu and Marathi.

Most of the videos developed during this campaign focused on a marital relationship, where the husband thinks he cannot possibly be infected with HIV. Most people think it can never happen to them and take unnecessary risks. This campaign helped people to talk about these issues because unless men wear condoms, even with their own wives, HIV & AIDS will continue to spread. The hypothesis of this campaign was that, barely 5% of Indian women have comprehensive knowledge about ways of preventing HIV & AIDS. It was felt that, women are often not in a social or economic position to insist on fidelity in marriage and relationships, demand condom use, or refuse sex to a partner who may pose a risk to their sexual health. 'What Kind of Man Are You?' is a path-breaking campaign because it encouraged more equal relationships between men and women to prevent the further spread of HIV & AIDS. It was able to spark a public dialogue about difficult but necessary issues like fidelity, protection from HIV & AIDS and communication within marriage. The campaign constructed it as a serious health and human rights issue. While popular perception might lead one to believe that most of these women are commercial sex workers. Official numbers indicate that sex workers constitute fewer than the overall female infections. Hence the reality is that the majority of women with HIV & AIDS in India have been infected by a husband or primary male partner!

### Men Make a Difference campaign

Gender equality and empowerment were considered as the key areas for the control of HIV & AIDS. Men were held responsible for their sexual and reproductive health. It is also stressed that men should not endanger their sexual partners. HIV control programmes have targeted men in many countries. Programmes were initiated to reduce high risk and number of partners among truck drivers like the Healthy Highways Project in India. The HIV epidemic is mainly heterosexual, with 70% of the infections occurring due to sexual contacts between males and females (UNAIDS, 2000). Three-fourths of the infections in India are due to the heterosexual transmission of the virus (NACO, 1999). Men Make a Difference was the title of the first year (2000–1) of a two-year campaign focusing on the role of men in the AIDS epidemic. This campaign aimed to involve men more fully in the effort against AIDS and to bring about a much-needed focus on men in national responses to the epidemic. All over the world, women find themselves at special risk of HIV infection because of their lack of power to determine where, when and how sex takes place. What is less recognised, however, is that the cultural beliefs and expectations that make this the case also heighten men's own vulnerability. Part of the effort to curb the AIDS epidemic included challenging harmful concepts of masculinity and changing many commonly held attitudes and behaviours, including the way men view risk and how boys are socialised to become men. Broadly speaking, men were expected to be physically strong, emotionally robust, daring and virile. Films signify this concept only when it states—'Those who care, know this is the right thing, condom always'.

*Yehi hai Sahi* (This is right) was a theme-based campaign. In one such short film in which a newlywed bridegroom delays the 'act' till his bride is comfortable. Thus, the tagline, 'Those who care know this is the right thing— Condom always!' Some of these expectations translate into ways of thinking and behaving that endanger the health and well-being of men and their sex partners. Other behaviours and attitudes, on the contrary, represent valuable potential that can be tapped by AIDS programme. Focusing the campaign on men also acknowledged the fact that men are often less likely to seek healthcare than women. But boys who are brought up to believe that 'real men don't get sick' often see themselves as invulnerable to illness or risk. This is reflected in the under-use of health services by men. All over the world, men tend to have more sex partners than women, including more extramarital partners, thereby increasing their own and their primary partners' risk of contracting HIV (UNAIDS, 2000). More men than women inject drugs and are therefore more likely to infect themselves and others through the use of unsterilised equipment. And many men who have sex with other men do not know how to protect themselves or their partners. Secrecy, stigma and shame surrounding HIV compound the effects of all these risk behaviours. The stigma surrounding HIV may prevent many men and women from acknowledging that they have become infected. *Men and AIDS – A Gendered Approach* (UNAIDS, 2000) elaborates that men have to play an important role in fighting the epidemic. It states that men engage in behaviour such as drinking, using illegal substances, or driving recklessly that puts their health at risk. Such kind of behaviour puts them at risk of HIV. While HIV transmission among women is growing, men including adolescent boys, continue to represent the majority of people living worldwide with HIV & AIDS. In some settings, men are less likely than women to pay attention to their sexual health and safety. Men are more likely than women to use alcohol and other substances that lead to unsafe sex and increase the risk of HIV transmission, and men are more likely to inject drugs, risking infection from needles and syringes contaminated with HIV. The report also points out HIV is more easily transmitted from men to women than vice versa. In addition, HIV-positive drug users who are mostly male can transmit the virus to both their drug partners and sex partners. A man with HIV is therefore likely to infect more people over a lifetime than an HIV-positive woman. Many men who have sex with men also have sex with women, their wives, or regular or occasional girlfriends. Hostility and misconceptions about sex between men have resulted in inadequate HIV prevention measures in many countries. The report urges the fathers and future fathers to consider the potential impact of their sexual behaviour on their partners and children. Men also need to take a greater role in caring for family members with HIV or AIDS.

## Sexual medicine: Reaching out to the masses

For many years in India, sexual pleasure has been depicted in various hues; darker and lighter, enraging and soothing. Sex was revered, worshipped, followed and yet tabooed, looked down upon. It was also considered a vice that one needs to protect oneself from. Nonetheless, sex continues to be talked about in hushed tones, not to be discussed beyond closed doors. In such a scenario, the good and ills about sex remain undisclosed. Men and women undergo great distress from sexual problems but help-seeking is vehemently avoided. When any help is sought, it is from friends, local healers and self-proclaimed doctors who promise guaranteed cure within 24 hours (Rao & Avasthi, 2008). With local media flashing such as posters, pamphlets etc., such attractive advertisements, the sufferers easily fall prey. To say the least, most of the people suffering from sexual problems never reach the 'doctor' to seek medical advice. This is especially true for our country. HIV prevalence in India is measured through the data coming out of the surveillance of antenatal and sexually transmitted disease clinics. Sexual medicine is not taught in any university in India. And the modern medical fraternity is overlooking it. As a result of which, unqualified and unregistered doctors doling out unnamed drugs are on the rise. Patients see advertisements on sexual medicines and go to them thinking such medicine is some sort of magic. Unfortunately, in India, section 33EEC of the Drugs and Cosmetics Act of 1940 exempts drugs manufactured by Vaidya's or hakims (traditional health practitioners). Thus, as long as the quack sells his medicine to patients who come to him of their own accord, no standards or safety regulations apply. A huge industry is thriving in India, which banks particularly on the taboos, myths about sexual health. Sexual medicine has made many inroads into India. We can find many posters, pamphlets and handouts pasted at every convenient corners in India. This may range from densely populated such as bus stands, railway stations, markets, etc. and to the least populated areas as well. This is developing into a very interesting field of research. Sex still being a taboo, and compound with sexual ailments, most of the population are keen to approach the 'doctors' that they come to know through the posters etc. From a sure-shot shot treatment *(shartiya ilaaj)* to any kind of sexual ailment being provided by the 'doctors', who could be a simple Registered Medical Practitioner (RMP) or any quack. Further, exhaustive research needs to be done in this area that can add to the body of knowledge in sexual health communication in India.

## Note

1  www.nacoonline.org/NACO/National_AIDS_Control_Program/Services_for_Preventi on/Condom_Promotion accessed on 18/01/2013.

# 6  Social construction of sexual citizenship

One of the paradoxes of Indian culture is that sexual desire is used to sell everything from soaps to motorbikes while sexuality of its masses is denied. Even as the Government of India has changed its position for abstinence-only-until-marital sex approach, sexually transmitted disease rates among young people keep soaring. The first step is to get honest about sex. The media is an important source of information and models of healthy sexuality for young people. It is in this background that this book attempts to understand the various facets of sexual health communication in India through its HIV & AIDS messages. The book also highlights the various ways in which sexual health gets constructed. This book can be considered as a contribution to existing body of knowledge on health communication and sexual health in India. Sexual health is an intricate and a multidimensional subject that has been addressed in different times and in different manners all over the world. During the Population Control Programme, it was addressed in a 'safe-guarding' mode, whose primary aim was only population control. The basic premise was to prevent people from producing more children. But HIV & AIDS had more to do with people refraining from sexual activities and thus constituted a 'regulatory' mode on sexual health. Starting with an initial response of denial by the Government of India, HIV & AIDS has come a long way. The initial belief was that it cannot spread in India because of strong family values and heterosexual lifestyles. HIV & AIDS kept spreading silently and by the time of initiation of the National AIDS Control Programme (NACP) almost all of the states of the country were affected to varying degrees. The blood transmission route, which was the least cause of HIV infection, was prioritised in approaches adopted by the government. Concentrating on high-risk population started during the NACP-II. Most of the campaigns either focused on HIV or STDs, but failed to highlight the linkages between them. NACO aimed to contain HIV ultimately through control of STDs. More focus was stressed on 'abstinence (A)' and 'behaviour change (B)' of the ABCD approach. The 'condom (C)' anyway existed since the population control programmes. In condom promotion, there is again a need to counter the strong belief amongst married women that it is only for birth control and they are safe from the epidemic. Sustained media campaigns need to be taken up to promote condom use where ever necessary as a mode of HIV prevention, rather than portraying it as a pleasure device. Female condoms also need to be promoted in a similar manner, where women can protect themselves in cases where men refuse to use condom. The lesbian, gay, bisexual and transgender (LGBT) groups in India have also been demanding separate spaces for themselves in the entire debate on HIV & AIDS. They have been vociferously demanding at various forums about their sexual rights, urging the government to understand and address issues related to their sexual health needs. Indeed, a controversy arose when one of the judges of high court endorsed the sexual rights of homosexuals better known as Article 377. It was the culmination of a successful fight against the provision in Section 377 of the Penal Code of India. Section 377 criminalised private consensual sex between adults of the same sex. This law had led to serious discrimination against people engaging in homosexual acts, who were subjected to frequent threats of prosecution by police. The law also has likely impeded the battle against HIV. The provision was read down in July 2009 after a sustained mass media campaign by activists known as the Voices Against 377. It brought together sexuality and LGBT organisations. The judgment transcended the LGBT issue with the implication of protection for all minorities and introduced for the first time in South Asia the idea of sexual citizenship. The supreme court of India in a landmark judgement on 6th September 2018 decriminalised section 377 of the Indian Penal Code and legalised consensual sexual relations among gay adults.

As Myhre & Flora (2000: 42) put it, 'HIV & AIDS campaigns originated in an atmosphere of public health urgency and fear'. Numerous campaigns have experimented with key strategies to overcome the obstacles to provide sexual health services to targeted populations. Social disapproval as well as intimidation can be tackled well by mobilising the community effectively (AIDS Alert, 2000; Alstead et al., 1999). Gearing up sexual health messages to specific subgroups of the population, by segmenting the audience and designing culture-specific messages would increase access to health services (Backer et al., 1992). Motivational media campaigns need to use clear, simple messages. Multiple media channels; and dissemination of positive images can increase awareness about the risks of being sexually active. This will help people indulging in risk behaviour to take preventive measures (Kirby et al., 1999). In all health communication programmes, the involvement of members of the target audience as educators, coordinators and programme developers are considered key to success (AIDS Alert, 2000). Sexual health campaigns will be most effective when the media are complemented by other activities at the individual, community and policy levels and when the campaign can be sustained over the long term (McGuire, 1989 as cited in Keller & Brown, 2002). The messages provided in safer sex or AIDS prevention media campaigns will get lost in the sea of competing messages that promote irresponsible and unhealthy sexual behaviours unless they are repeated extensively and reinforced by service providers and public policy (Keller & Brown, 2002; Vemula & Rao, 2016). In addition, there needs to be political leadership that provides a vision for combating the epidemic. Each community's needs must be assessed for their 'community readiness' to implement a comprehensive programme that includes services to prevent the epidemic. It can no more be 'top down'. The 'bottom up' approach cannot also be based on the fact of information overload on the marginalised.

Sexual health as a concept is still evolving. It still is used in diverse ways both in academia as well as in the policy publications. What is needed is a strong critical and interdisciplinary reflection on the conceptualisation and the application of the concept everywhere (Sandfort & Ehrhardt, 2004). In order to be effective, sexual health promotion needs to be informed by an interdisciplinary understanding of sexuality that requires scientific understanding. In his *History of Sexuality*, Foucault stated that sexuality was produced through the strategies of power-knowledge. The state becomes the storehouse of the knowledge that gets disseminated through its institutions. In India, health is a subject addressed by the central government. Thus, HIV & AIDS also comes under their purview. Starting from National STD Control Programme, the Government of India has held control over the manner in which the concept of sexual health gets formulated. These attempts were largely influenced by the Western donor agencies, which have been funding and have become the 'ideology' based on which sexual health messages were created and disseminated in the entire country. Starting from a biomedical mode of message dissemination to moral mode of dissemination, parallels can be drawn on the manner in which countries all around the world were addressing the issue of HIV & AIDS. All the countries around the world based their communication strategies on Information, Education and Communication (IEC) mode for a long time, which was later to be known as top-down. As time passed, and as the approach of the funding agencies diverted to individual behaviour change, all the countries shifted their approach to Behaviour Change Communication (BCC), without realising if it would work or not. This approach was later known as 'bottom-up'. Ambiguities still exist about who are at the bottom!

The comparative analysis taken up in this book clearly outlines this dilemma that different countries face regarding HIV & AIDS. Each country has its own set of sub-populations that needs attention and the messages need to be targeted at them. Netherlands and Finland are more concerned about MSMs and migrant populations, whereas countries like Thailand are worried about the population who work in 'sex establishments'. In most of the countries, safe sex practices are often seen as social problems of the poor and the marginalised. Thus, most of the developing countries are diverting their energies and funds to address these sub-populations from the general population. This could be termed as a discriminatory approach of the funders and the states that implements such interventions. Netherlands and Finland have fewer sub-populations to worry about in comparison to other developing countries. That's the reason they are investing in development of vaccine for HIV. Sexual health education needs to be understood in a multidisciplinary way before it is introduced at the school level. A proper understanding of the cultural, structural factors that define the existence of the epidemic need to be understood, before sex education about a responsible sexual citizen is imparted. The next section elaborates on the aspects of sexual health behaviour and responsible sexual citizenship, both aspects which are inherently necessary factors for a country to progress. The resources and energies that are invested by the state can be diverted to other avenues, if the people behave responsibly in terms of their sexual health.

## Deconstructing sexual citizenship

The WHO proceedings on *Promotion of Sexual Health: A Recommendation for Action* states that 'responsible sexual behaviour' is expressed at individual, interpersonal and community levels. It is characterised by autonomy, mutuality, honesty, respectfulness, consent, protection, pursuit of pleasure and wellness (WHO, 2001:8). This definition elaborates further that a person who exhibits responsible sexual behaviour does not intend to cause harm, and refrains from exploitation, harassment, manipulation and discrimination. It also determines the role of a community, which also could mean the state, which promotes responsible sexual behaviour by providing the knowledge, resources and rights for individuals to engage in such practices. The combination of sexual rights as a contested concept and the increasing usage of the language of citizenship in sexual politics, underlines the need for a critical analysis of its meaning and value as a concept. There are competing claims for what are defined as sexual rights and lack of rights, reflecting not only differences in how sexuality is conceptualised but also the fact that there is no singular agreed definition of sexual citizenship. Sexual citizenship discourse began by noting three components of citizenship: civil, political and social. In particular, theorists of sexual citizenship argue that citizenship claims are based on heterosexual and male privilege. The theoretical construct of sexual citizenship is based more on metaphorical notions. It does pertain to the legal regulations of sexuality: sexual practices, sexual speech, public entitlements (welfare) and marriage (Robson & Kessler, 2009). As seen with the concept of sexual health, there is no agreed-upon definition of 'sexual citizenship' (Richardson, 2000). It is sometimes used as a collection of legal or political rights. In other instances, the emphasis is on the relation of the consumption of goods and services to sexual practices and identities. Citizenship is premised on institutionalised heterosexuality, which lacks legal protection for gays and lesbians from discrimination or harassment. They have limited political rights and have limited access to 'full social citizenship', even in the realms of welfare, education, parenting, employment and housing (Richardson, 2000). The LGBT groups are tolerated as 'partial citizens'. They have to conform to the condition 'that they remain in the private sphere and do not seek public recognition or membership in the political community'. (Richardson, 1998: 89).

> With homosexuality viewed as a threat to the nation-state, gays and lesbians are excluded from the 'construction of "nation" and nationality'. It

needs to be noted that increasing use of the language of sexual citizenship is in contrast to the language of sexual liberation.

(Richardson, 2000)

The very concept of sexual citizen tends to breach the public-private divide. Thus, it brings the sexuality into the public sphere (Weeks, 1998). The claim to sexual citizenship arises from cultural shifts that are undermining traditional hierarchical relationships. The relationship between individuals and the state—the concept of citizenship has little relevance without a nation. It can be argued that sexual citizenship relates to Foucault's analysis of governmentality—government practices that monitor and shape individuals' conduct—and self-discipline—the ways in which individuals act upon themselves (Robson & Kessler, 2009). When citizenship transcends national boundaries, new questions arise, such as which government or international entity is regulating individuals. Foucauldian claims that citizenship has a disciplinary function as 'intuitively persuasive', but maintains that 'rights and citizenship retain an unruly and unpredictable political and social edge'. (Cossman, 2007). In this sense, discipline is 'resistable'. Historically, citizenship has been built on exclusions through binary divisions, with two primary axes: private/public and active/passive. Sexual citizenship articulates sexuality in the public sphere, by way of claims for rights and participation, while also claiming a 'right to spaces for sub-cultural life' (Stychin, 1998). Traditionally, states perpetuate traditional dominant ideologies of the sexual as individual, personal, private, definitively divorced from material structures and power relations. Yet, as merely passing references to the civil, political and social rights of various sexual minorities and the marketing of sexual imagery and commodities make clear, this is manifestly not the case (Evans, 2010).

HIV prevalence in India is measured through the data coming out of the surveillance of antenatal and sexually transmitted disease clinics. These data cannot provide real insight into where transmission is occurring or guide programme strategy. The factors that influence the Indian epidemic are the size, behaviours and disease burdens of high-risk groups, and their interaction with sub-populations. The interplay of these forces has resulted in substantial epidemics in several pockets of many Indian states that could potentially ignite sub-epidemics in other, currently low prevalence, parts of the country (Chandrasekharan et al., 2006). Unless and until HIV is contained, it will continue to have consequences for India's development. India's national response to HIV began in 1992 and has shown early success in some states. The priority was to build on those successes by increasing prevention coverage of high-risk groups to saturation level, enhancing access and uptake of care and treatment services, ensuring systems and capacity for evidence-based programming, and building in-country technical and managerial capacity. Peter Piot, the director of UNAIDS aptly sums up the HIV & AIDS scenario in India wherein he states that the challenges India faces to overcome HIV & AIDS are enormous. He also at the same time emphasises on the ample quantities of all the resources that are needed to achieve universal access to HIV prevention and treatment that would aid in defeating AIDS. This will require a significant intensification of efforts, in India, just as in the rest of the world (UNAIDS 2006 cited in Kodandapani & Alpert, 2007).

## Communication campaigns on sexual health: Way forward

Myths, misinformation and misconceptions still abound about HIV & AIDS. It is still associated with death, dirty, bad and morally wrong actions. The general impression that 'everyone is doing it' and it is OK to have sex in pre- and post-marital situations has got an impetus largely due to liberal media and easy access to money and revolution in information technology. In such a kind of a scenario, communication becomes a cross-cutting and integral strategic intervention in all components of HIV & AIDS prevention. There must be comprehensive sex education (awareness) at the school level. But the problem in Indian languages is that it does not have a clinical vocabulary for discussing sex, sexuality and sexually transmitted diseases.

As this book has attempted to show, the issue is not only about HIV & AIDS, but also about the politics of the human sexual relationships that serve as the prime carrier of HIV. This politics has largely been ignored. The primary objective of the HIV & AIDS campaigns is to limit the epidemicity of the disease. What is needed is a value orientation rather than information orientation because knowledge is a necessary but not sufficient condition for prevention of HIV & AIDS. This implies that campaigns should be designed not just to increase knowledge about HIV & AIDS but also stress upon attitude and behaviour change. There must also be emphasis on improving gender sensitivity on the part of both men and women and on improving the negotiating skills of women in casual sexual encounters. Several Communication Needs Assessments (CNA) studies have noted the influence of gate-keepers. Till date most of the HIV & AIDS campaigns have focussed mostly on film and sports personalities, but there is a need to go beyond and make appeal to different sets of audiences. Non-mass media approaches need to be looked at much more closely. Communication for HIV & AIDS requires an insightful behavioural analysis. Since talking about sex is personal, social sensitivity is the prime concern. Individual and socio-cultural aspects play a very important role in designing the messages. Changing behaviour (in contrast to changing knowledge) requires formative research that focuses on in-depth behavioural analysis—that is research to uncover why current behaviours persist and why new behaviours are resisted. Tackling HIV & AIDS also requires an active and coordinated intersectoral involvement, particularly education and industry that can magnify the impact of health sector programming. A thorough documentation of the behavioural interventions will definitely aid in planning communication campaigns. As Singhal & Rogers (2003:73) state that HIV is not a common everyday infectious disease. It cannot be transmitted in contaminated water and food, like cholera or typhoid. The virus cannot be transmitted by an insect, as are plague and malaria. HIV is not transmitted through air, like influenza and tuberculosis, nor through physical touch, like fungal infections. HIV transmission usually requires the active participation of an individual in activities in which bodily fluids (semen or blood) are exchanged. Theoretically, HIV's spread can thus be controlled. Communication strategies must, therefore, be firmly based in the cultural realities of the behaviour patterns and belief systems of India. They should also be able address the constraints and limitations that an individual faces while attempting to initiate new behaviours, within the social structures and personal relationships such as social norms, perceptions of self-efficacy, and power inequalities in relationships.

# Declarations and commitments on HIV & AIDS

# Interview guide

a   How has the concept of 'sexual health' evolved in India in the context of HIV & AIDS?
b   What were the initial understandings of the 'institutions' like NACP/ NACO in conceptualising the concept of sexual health for the Indian population?
c   Which social, cultural and religious messages were taught to you? In which ways they influenced the way you learned, experienced and defined the normative sexual health practices?
d   How various factors have as morality, faithfulness and dedication got weaved into the sexual health messages?
e   How have you related your own understandings of sexuality to the work undertaken by you with regards to sexual health?
f   Why and how did the condom get repositioned in HIV and AIDS campaign after its lack of success during the family planning programmes?
g   Do you think institutions set the parameters for normative sexual health?

# References

Adams, J. (1995). *Risk*. London: UCL Press.

Aggleton, P., & Campbell, C. (2000). 'Working with young people: Towards an agenda for sexual health'. *Sexual and Relationship Therapy*, 15(3). 283–296.

Aggleton, P., Parker, R., & Malawa, M. (2003). *Stigma, Discrimination and HIV & AIDS in Latin America and the Caribbean*. Washington, DC: Inter-American Development Bank.

AIDS Alert. (2000). *Youth Programs Take Pop-Culture Approach*. AHC Media LLC. Retrieved from High Beam Research: www.highbeam.com/doc/1G1-63985277.html.

Airhihenbuwa, C.O., & Obregon, R. (2000). 'A critical assessment of theories/models used in health communication for HIV & AIDS'. *Journal of Health Communication*, 5(Supplement). 5–15.

Allen, M., Hunter, J.E., & Donohue, W.A. (1989). 'Meta-analysis of self-report data on the effectiveness of public speaking anxiety treatment techniques'. *Communication Education*, 38(1). 54–76.

Alstead, M., Campsmith, M., Halley, C.S., Hartfield, K., Goldbaum, G., & Wood, R.W. (1999). 'Developing, implementing, and evaluating a condom promotion program targeting sexually active adolescents'. *AIDS Education and Prevention*, 11. 497–512.

Altheide, D.L. (1996). *Qualitative Media Analysis*. London: SAGE Publications.

Anders, J.T., Antonius-Smits, C., Cabezas, A.L., Campbell, S., Davidson, J.O.C., Fernandez, N. ..., & Mohammed, P. (1999). *Sun, Sex, and Gold: Tourism and Sex Work in the Caribbean*. Boulder, CO: Rowman and Littlefield.

Armstrong, D. (1995). 'The rise of surveillance medicine'. *Sociology of Health & Illness*, 17(3). 393–404.

Atkin, C. (1981). 'Mass media information campaign effectiveness'. In Rice, R. & Paisley, W. (Eds.) *Public Communication Campaigns* (pp. 265–280). Thousand Oaks, CA: SAGE.

Avert. (2011). 'Avert's HIV and AIDS media gallery'. Retrieved from www.avert.org accessed on 21/12/2012.

Baber, K.M., & Allen, K.R. (1992). 'Women's sexualities'. In Baber, K.M. & Allen, K.R. (Eds.) *Women and Families: Feminist Reconstructions* (pp. 61–101). Thousand Oaks, CA: SAGE.

Backer, T.E., Rogers, E.M., & Sopory, P. (1992). *Designing Health Communication Campaigns: What Works*. Newbury Park, CA: SAGE Publications.

Bandura, A. (1986). *Social Foundations of Thought and Action: A Social Cognitive Approach*. Englewood Cliffs, NJ: Prentice Hall.

Barrett, M. (1991). 'Sexual health education: Can a new vision avoid repetition of past errors?' *SIECCAN Journal*, 6(4). 3–15.

Barthes, R. (1977). *Rhetoric of the Image*. New York: Hill & Wang.

Beatrice Bean'E, R., Bockting, W.O., Rosser, B.S., Miner, M., & Coleman, E. (2002). 'The sexual health model: Application of a sexological approach to HIV prevention'. *Health Education Research*, 17(1). 43–57.

Bentley, M.E., Spratt, K., Shepherd, M.E., Gangakhedkar, R.R., Thilakavathi, S., Bollinger, R. C., & Mehendale, S.M. (1998). 'HIV testing and counselling among men attending sexually transmitted disease clinics in Pune, India: Changes in condom use and sexual behavior over time'. *AIDS*, 12. 1869–1877.

Berger, P., & Luckmann, T. (1966). *The Social Construction of Reality: A Treatise in the Sociology of Knowledge*. Harmondsworth: Penguin Books.

Berne, L., & Huberman, B. (1999). *European Approaches to Adolescent Sexual Behavior and Responsibility*. Washington, DC: Advocates for Youth.

Bill and Melinda Gates Foundation. (2009). *Managing HIV Prevention from the Ground Up: Avahan's Experience with Peer Led Outreach at Scale in India*. New Delhi: Bill and Melinda Gates Foundation.

Blumer, H. (1971). 'Social problems as collective behavior'. *Social Problems*, 18(3). 298–306.

Bockting, W.O., Rosser, B.R.S., & Coleman, E. (1999). 'Transgender HIV prevention: community involvement and empowerment'. *International Journal of Transgenderism*, 3(1/2). Retrieved from www.symposion.com/ijt.

Boesten, J., & Poku, N. (2009). *Gender and HIV & AIDS: Critical Perspectives from the Developing World*. Ashgate Publishing Company. Retrieved from http://books.google.co.in/books.

Bogdan, R.C., & Biklen, S.K. (1982). *Qualitative Research for Education: An Introduction to Theory and Methods*. Boston: Allyn and Bacon, Inc.

Bose, A. (1998). *From Population to People*, Volume I & II (pp. 574). Delhi: BR Publishing Corporation.

Breakthrough. (2005). 'Campaign press release'. Retrieved from http://breakthrough.tv/explore/campaign/what-kind-of-man-are-you accessed on 22/11/2010.

Brown, J., Chapman, S., & Lupton, D. (1996). 'Infinitesimal risk as public health crisis: news media coverage of a doctor–patient HIV contact tracing investigation'. *Social Science and Medicine*, 43(12).1685–1695.

Burr, V. (1995). *An Introduction to Social Constructionism*. London: Routledge.

Chandrasekaran, P., Dallabetta, G., Loo, V., Rao, S., Gayle, H., & Alexander, A. (2006). 'Containing HIV & AIDS in India: The unfinished agenda'. *The Lancet Infectious Diseases*, 6. 508–521.

Chaudhuri, N.C. (1966). *The Continent of Circe: An Essay on the Peoples of India*. (pp. 320). New York: Oxford University Press.

Cheng, S. (2005). 'Popularising purity: Gender, sexuality and nationalism in HIV & AIDS prevention for South Korean youths'. *Asia Pacific Viewpoint*, 46(1).7–20.

Chhabra, R. (2007). 'National AIDS Control Programme: A critique'. *Economic and Political Weekly*, XLII(2). 103–108.

Chiwara, T.B. (2012). *The Impact of Billboards on HIV and AIDS Awareness in Zimbabwe*. (Doctoral dissertation). Stellenbosch, South Africa: University of Stellenbosch.

Clarke, K. (2002). 'Policing silence, practicing invisibility: Migrants living with HIV & AIDS in Finland'. *Social Work in Europe*, 9(3). 20–27.

Cohen, D. (2002). *Human Capital and the HIV Epidemic in Sub-Saharan Africa.* Geneva: ILO Programme on HIV & AIDS and the World of Work. Retrieved from www.oit.org/wcmsp5/groups/public/—ed_protect/—protrav/—ilo_aids/documents/pu blication/wcms_117152.pdf.

Cohen, S. (2003). 'Beyond slogans: Lessons from Uganda's ABC experience', *The Guttmacher Report on Public Policy.* Retrieved from www.agi-usa.org/pubs/ ib2004no2.html.

Coleman, E. (2002). 'Promoting sexual health and responsible sexual behavior: An introduction'. *Journal of Sex Research*, 39(1). 3–6.

Colle, R. (2002). 'Threads of development communication'. In Servaes, J. (Ed.), *Communication and Development for Social Change.* (pp. 96–157). Paris: UNESCO.

Collins, J., & Rau, B. (2000). *AIDS in the Context of Development*, Geneva: UNRISD and UNAIDS (Paper No.4).

Connelly, M. J. (2009). *Fatal Misconception: The Struggle to Control World Population.* Boston, MA: Harvard University Press.

Connelly, M., & Macleod, C. (2003). 'Waging war: Discourses of HIV & AIDS in South African media'. *African Journal of Aids Research*, 2(1). 1–11.

Conrad, P., & Barker, K. (2010). 'The social construction of illness: Key insights and policy implications'. *Journal of Health and Social Behavior*, 51(S). S67–S79.

Correa, S. & Reichmann, R. (1994). *Population and Reproductive Rights: Feminist Perspectives from the South.* London: Zed Books Ltd. and New Delhi: Women's Association and Dawn.

Cossman, B. (2007). *Sexual Citizens: The Legal and Cultural Regulation of Sex and Belonging.* Stanford, CA: Stanford University Press.

Cutler, D.M., Fung, W., Kremer, M., & Singhal, M. (2007). *Mosquitoes: The Long-Term Effects of Malaria Eradication in India.* Cambridge: Harvard University, John F. Kennedy School of Government.

Daily Pioneer. (2013). Retrieved from www.dailypioneer.com/nation/funds-for-nacp -phase-iv-approved.html accessed on 13/07/2017.

Daniel, H., & Parker, R. (1993). *Sexuality, Politics and AIDS in Brazil.* London: Falmer Press.

De Waal, A. (2003). 'How will HIV & AIDS transform African governance?' *African Affairs*, 102(406). 1–23.

Denzin, N.K. (1989). *The Research Act* (3rd Ed. ). Englewood Cliffs, NJ: Prentice Hall.

Donahue, J. (1998). *Community-Based Economic Support for Households Affected by HIV & AIDS.* Arlington, VA: USAID, HIV & AIDS Division.

Duckett, M., & Orkin, A. (1989). 'AIDS-related migration and travel policies and restrictions–A global survey', *AIDS* 3(suppl. 1). S231–252.

Dutta, M.J. (2006). 'Theoretical approaches to entertainment education campaigns: A subaltern critique'. *Health Communication*, 20(3). 221–231.

Dutta-Bergman, M.J. (2004). 'The unheard voices of Santalis: Communicating about health from the margins of India'. *Communication Theory*, 14(3). 237–263.

Edwards, W.M., & Coleman, E. (2004). 'Defining sexual health: A descriptive overview'. *Archives of Sexual Behavior*, 33(3). 189–195.

Emmons, K.M. (2000). 'Behavioral and social science contributions to the health of adults in the United States'. In B. Smedley & S.L. Syme (Eds.), *Promoting Health: Intervention Strategies from Social and Behavioral Research* (pp. 254–321). Institute of Medicine, Washington, DC: National Academy Press.

Evans, D.T. (2010). *Sexual Citizenship: The Material Construction of Sexualities*. London: Routledge.

Farmer, P., Connors, M., & Simmons, J. (1996). *Women, Poverty and AIDS: Sex, Drugs and Structural Violence*. (Eds). Monroe, ME: Common Courage Press.

Fee, E., & Fox, D.M. (1988). *AIDS: The Burdens of History*. Berkeley, CA: University of California Press.

Ferrante, J. (1988). 'Biomedical versus cultural constructions of abnormality: The case of idiopathic hirsutism in the United States'. *Culture, Medicine and Psychiatry*, 22 (2). 219–238.

Finnegan, J.R., & Viswanath, K. (1997). 'Communication theory and health behavior change: The media studies framework'. In Glanz, K., Lewis, F.M., & Rimer, B.K. (Eds.), *Health Behavior and Health Education: Theory, Research and Practice* (pp. 313–341). San Francisco: Jossey-Bass.

Flay, B.R. (1987). 'Mass media and smoking cessation: a critical review'. *American Journal of Public Health*, 77(2). 153–160.

Flay, B.R., & Burton, D. (1990). 'Effective mass communication strategies for health campaigns'. In Atkin, C. and Wallack, L. (Eds). *Mass Communication and Public Health: Complexities and Conflicts* (pp. 129–146). Newbury Park, CA: SAGE.

Flora, J.A., & Maibach, E.W. (1990). 'Cognitive responses to AIDS information: The effects of issue involvement and message appeal'. *Communication Research*, 17(6). 759–774.

Foreman, M. (2004). 'Males, men and MSM'. *Pukaar*, 45. 3–4.

Foss, S., & Griffin, C. (1995). 'Beyond persuasion: A proposal for invitational rhetoric'. *Communication Monographs*, 62(1). 2–18.

Foucault, M. (1978). *The History of Sexuality* (French original 1976). Harmondsworth: Penguin Books.

Foucault, M. (1979). 'Ideology and consciousness'. *Governmentality*, (6). 5–21.

Freimuth, V.S. (1990). 'The chronically uninformed: Closing the knowledge gap in health'. In Ray, T.E.B. & Donohew, L. (Eds.), *Communication and Health: Systems and Applications* (pp. 171–186). Hillsdale, NJ: Lawrence Erlbaum Associates, Inc.

Freire, P. (1976). *Pedagogy of the Oppressed*. London: Penguin Books.

Gastaldo, D. (1997). 'Is health education good for you? Re-thinking health education through the concept of bio-power'. In: Petersen, A. & Bunton, R. (Eds.). *Foucault, Health and Medicine*. London: Routledge.

George, A. (1997). *Sexual Behavior and Sexual Negotiation among Poor Women and Men in Mumbai: An Exploratory Study*. Vadodara, Gujarat, India: SAHAJ Society for Health Alternatives.

Gergen, K.J. (1985). 'The social constructionist movement in modern psychology'. *American Psychologist*, 40(3). 266–275.

Giami, A. (2002). 'Sexual health: The emergence, development, and diversity of a concept'. *Annual Review of Sex Research*, 13(1). 1–35.

Giddens, A. (1999). 'The Reith Lectures: Risk'. *BBC News Online*. Retrieved from http://news.bbc.co.uk/hi/english/static/events/reith_99/week2/week2.Htm accessed on 07/2018.

Gilmore, N., & Somerville, M.A. (1994). 'Stigmatization, scapegoating and discrimination in sexually transmitted diseases: Overcoming "them" and "us"'. *Social Science & Medicine*, 39(9). 1339–1358.

Go, V.F., Johnson, S.C., Bentley, M.E., Sivaram, S., Srikrishnan, A.K., Celentano, D. D., & Solomon, S. (2003). 'Crossing the threshold: Engendered definitions of socially acceptable domestic violence in Chennai, India'. *Culture, Health & Sexuality*, 5(5). 393–408.

Goswami, S. (2007). *Media and Communication in Post-Independence India*. Salford, UK: The Media, Communication and Cultural Studies Association.

Green, E.C. (2001). 'The impact of religious organizations in promoting HIV/AIDS'. *CCIH Forum*, 11(October). 2–11.

Green, E.C., Halperin, D.T., Nantulya, V., & Hogle, J.A. (2006). 'Uganda's HIV prevention success: The role of sexual behavior change and the national response'. *AIDS and Behavior*, 10(4). 335–346.

Greener, R. (2002). 'AIDS and macroeconomic impact'. In Forsyth, S. (Ed.). *State of The Art: AIDS and Economics* (pp. 49–55). Washington, DC: IAEN.

Gupta, G.R. (2000). 'Gender, sexuality, and HIV & AIDS: The what, the why, and the how'. In *Plenary Address*, XIIIth International AIDS Conference, Durban, South Africa, July (Vol. 12).

Guttman, N. (2000). *Public Health Communication Interventions: Values and Ethical Dilemmas*. Thousand Oaks, CA: SAGE.

Hacker, J.S. (2002). *The Divided Welfare State*. New York: Cambridge University Press.

Hafstad, A., & Aarø L.E. (1997). 'Activating interpersonal influence through provocative appeals: Evaluation of a mass media-based antismoking campaign targeting adolescents'. *Health Communication*, 9(3). 253–272.

Hantrais, L. (1996). 'Social research update'. *Comparative Research Methods*, 13(4).

Hart, G., & Wellings, K. (2002). 'Sexual behaviour and its medicalisation: In sickness and in health'. *British Medical Journal*, 324(7342). 896.

Hoffman, L. (1990). 'Constructing realities: An art of lenses'. *Family Process*, 29(1). 1–12.

Holzner, B. (1968). *Reality Construction in Society*. Cambridge, MA: Schenkman Publishing Company.

Hornik, R. (1989). 'Channel effectiveness in development communication programs'. In Rice, R. & Atkin, C. (Eds.). *Public Communication Campaigns* (2nd Ed. ). Beverly Hills, CA: SAGE.

Huber, J.T., & Gillapsy, M.L. (1998). 'Social Constructs and Disease: Implications for a Controlled Vocabulary for HIV & AIDS'. *Library Trends*, 47(2). 190–208.

Indian Council for Medical Research (ICMR). (2002). *Bulletin*, 32(11 & 12).

Ingle, H., & Vemula, R.K. (2012). 'Representation and social construction of HIV and AIDS in the mainstream Hindi cinema in India: A study on the discourses of normative sexual health'. *Journal of Global Communication*, 5(2). 97–105.

International Conference on Population and Development (ICPD). (1994). *Conference Report*. Document A/Conf. 171/13, New York: United Nations.

Johnson, J.D., & Meischke, H. (1993). 'A comprehensive model of cancer-related information seeking applied to magazines'. *Human Communication Research*, 19(3). 343–367.

Joint United Nations Programme on HIV and AIDS (UNAIDS). (1999). 'Epidemiological fact sheet on Uganda'. Retrieved from http://refkol.ro/gtp/2000s/10/uganda.pdf.

Joint United Nations Programme on HIV and AIDS (UNAIDS). (2000). 'Men and AIDS - a gendered approach'. *World AIDS Campaign*. Retrieved from http://data.unaids.org/pub/report/2000/20000622_wac_men_en.pdf.

Joint United Nations Programme on HIV and AIDS (UNAIDS). (2001). *HIV & AIDS and Communication for Behavior and Social Change: Programme Experiences, Examples, and the Way Forward*. Geneva: International Workshop UNAIDS.

Joint United Nations Programme on HIV and AIDS (UNAIDS). (2006). *Report on the Global AIDS Epidemic*. Geneva: UNAIDS, Retrieved from http://data.unaids. org/pub/GlobalReport/2006/2006_gr-executivesummary_en.pdf.

Joint United Nations Programme on HIV and AIDS (UNAIDS). (2012). *Global Report: UNAIDS Report on the Global AIDS Epidemic 2012*. Geneva: UNAIDS, Retrieved from www.unaids.org/en/media/unaids/contentassets/documents/epidemiol ogy/2012.

Joint United Nations Programme on HIV and AIDS (UNAIDS) & World Health Organization (WHO). (2000). 'Guidelines for second generation HIV surveillance'. Retrieved from www.who.int/hiv/pub/surveillance/en/cds_edc_2000_5.pdf accessed on 24/3/2012.

Kalipeni, E., Craddock, S., Oppong, J., & Ghosh, J. (2004). *HIV & AIDS in Africa: Beyond Epidemiology*. (Eds). Oxford: Blackwell.

Kaplan, R.M. (1990). 'Behavior as the central outcome in health care'. *American Psychologist*, 45(11). 1211–1220.

Karpf, A. (1988). *Doctoring the Media: The Reporting of Health and Medicine*. London: Routledge.

Keinsten, K. (1989). 'Living with AIDS: Social construction and the long haul'. *Working Paper in Program in Science*, Cambridge, MA: Technology and Society, MIT.

Keller, S.N., & Brown, J.D. (2002). 'Media interventions to promote responsible sexual behavior'. *The Journal of Sex Research*, 39, (1). 67–72.

Kimmel, D.C., & Moody, H.R. (1990). 'Ethical issues in gerontological research and services'. In Birren, J.E. & Schaie, K.W. (Eds.). *Handbook of the Psychology of Aging* (3rd ed.) (pp. 489–501). Orlando, FL: Academic Press.

Kirby, D. (2002). 'Antecedents of adolescent initiation of sex, contraceptive use, and pregnancy'. *American Journal of Health Behaviour*, 26(6). 473–485.

Kirby, K.C., Marlowe, D.B., Festlinger, D.S., Garvey, K.A., & LaMonaca, V. (1999). 'Community reinforcement training for family and significant others of drug abusers: A unilateral intervention to increase treatment entry of drug users'. *Drug and Alcohol Dependence*, 56(1). 85–96.

Klugman, B. (1990). 'The politics of contraception in South Africa'. *Women's Studies International Forum*, 13(3). 261–271. Retrieved from www.researchgate.net/publica tion/294651353_South_African_women%27s_experiences_of_contraception_and_co ntraceptive_services.

Kodandapani, K., & Alpert, P.T. (2007). 'AIDS in India: When denial kills'. *Home, Health Care Management & Practice*, 20(1). 21–26.

Kovács, J. (1998). 'The concept of health and disease'. *Medicine, Health Care and Philosophy*, 1(1). 31–39.

Kress, G., & van Leeuwen, T. (2001). *Multimodal Discourse: The Modes and Media of Contemporary Communication*. London: Arnold.

Kumar, P. (2000). 'The National AIDS Control Programme (1,2,3)'. Retrieved from http://infochangeindia.org/hivonline/response_1.php.

Kvasny, L., & Chong, J. (2008). 'The ABC approach and the feminization of HIV & AIDS in the Sub-Saharan Africa'. In Wickramasinghe, N. & Geisler, E. (Eds.). *Encyclopedia of Healthcare Information Systems* (pp. 10–15). Hershey, PA: Medical Information Science Reference.

Lambert, H. (1998) 'Methods and meanings in anthropological, epidemiological and clinical encounters: The case of sexually transmitted disease and HIV control and prevention in India'. *Tropical Medicine and International Health*, 3(12). 1002–1010.

Lambert, H. (2001). 'Not talking about sex in India: Indirection and the communication of bodily intention'. In Hendry, J. & Watson, B. (Eds.) *An Anthropology of Indirect Communication.* London: Routledge.

Lambert, H., & Wood, K. (2005). 'A comparative analysis of communication about sex, health and sexual health in India and South Africa: Implications for HIV prevention'. *Culture, Health and Sexuality,* 7(6). 527–541.

Leheny, D. (1995). 'A political economy of Asian sex tourism'. *Annals of Tourism Research,* 22(2). 367–384.

Lerner, D. (1958). *The Passing of Traditional Society: Modernizing the Middle East.* Glencoe, NY: Free Press.

Levine, M. (1992). 'The implications of constructionist theory for social research on the AIDS epidemic among gay men'. In Herdt, G. & Lindenbaum, S. (Eds.) (pp. 185–198). *The Time of AIDS.* Newbury Park, CA: SAGE.

Levine, P. (1994). 'Venereal disease, prostitution, and the politics of empire: The case of British India', *Journal of the History of Sexuality,* 4(4). 579–602.

Lewis, L.J. (2004). 'Examining sexual health discourses in a racial/ethnic context'. *Archives of Sexual Behavior,* 33(3). 223–234.

Lottes, I. (2000). 'New perspectives in sexual health'. In Lottes, I. & Kontula, O. (Eds.). *New Views on Sexual Health: The Case of Finland* (pp. 7–29). Helsinki: The Population Research Institute.

Lottes, I. (2002). 'Sexual health policies in other industrialized, countries: Are there lessons for the United States?' *The Journal of Sex Research,* 39(1). 79–83.

Low-Beer, D., & Stoneburner, R.L. (2003). 'Behaviour and communication change in reducing HIV: Is Uganda unique?' *African Journal of AIDS Research*2003, 2(1). 9–21.

Lupton, D. (1993). 'AIDS risk and heterosexuality in the Australian press'. *Discourse & Society,* 4(3). 307–328.

Malcolm, A., Aggleton, P., Bronfman, M., Galvao, J., Mane, P., & Verrall, J. (1998). 'HIV-related stigmatization and discrimination: Its forms and contexts'. *Critical Public Health,* 8(4). 347–370.

Malikhao, P. (2005). 'HIV & AIDS prevention campaigns from a Thai Buddhist perspective'. *Media Development,* 52(2). 57–62.

Mann, J. (1987). 'Statement at an informal briefing on AIDS to the 42nd Session of the United Nations General Assembly', 20 October, New York.

Marshall, A.A., & McKeon, J.K. (1996). 'Reaching the unreachable: Educating and motivating women living in poverty'. In Ray, E.B. (Ed.). *Communication and Disenfranchisement* (pp. 137–155). Mahwah, NJ: Lawrence Erlbaum Associates.

Martin, J.N., & Nakayama, T.K. (1999). 'Thinking dialectically about culture and communication'. *Communication Theory,* 9(1). 1–25.

McEwen, J., MartiniC.J.M., & WilkinsN. (1983). *Participation in Health.* London: Croom Helm.

McGuire, W.J. (1989). 'Theoretical foundations of campaigns'. In Rice, R.E. & Atkin, C.K. (Eds.). *Public Communication Campaigns* (pp. 43–65). Newbury Park, CA: SAGE.

Melkote, S.R., & Steeves, H.L. (2001). *Communication for Development in the Third World* (2nd Ed. ). New Delhi: SAGE.

Meyer, A.J., Nash, J.D., McAlister, A.L., Maccoby, N., & Farquhar, J.W. (1980). 'Skills training in a cardiovascular health education campaign'. *Journal of Consulting and Clinical Psychology,* 48(2). 129.

Mies, M. (1983). 'Towards a methodology for feminist research'. In Bowles, G. & Klein, R.D. (Eds.). *Theories of Women's Studies* (pp. 117–140). London: Routledge and Kegan Paul.

Mitra, P. (2004). 'India at the crossroads: Battling the HIV & AIDS pandemic'. *The Washington Quarterly*, 27(4). 95–107.

Mohammed, S.K. (2003). 'The Ugandan response to HIV & AIDS: Some lessons for India'. *National Medical Journal of India*, 16(2). 262–269.

Mukherji, S., Priyadarshi, M., Singh, S., & World Bank. (2006). *Communication in Public Health Programs: The Leprosy Project in India*. New Delhi: The World Bank.

Mutangadura, G.B. (2000). *Household Welfare Impacts of Adult Females in Zimbabwe: Implications for Policy and Program Development*. Paper presented at the AIDS and Economics Symposium IAEN, Durban, South Africa.

Myhre, S.L., & Flora, J.A. (2000). 'HIV & AIDS communication campaigns: Progress and prospects'. *Journal of Health Communication*, 5(sup1). 29–45.

Nath, A. (2009). 'HIV & AIDS and Indian youth: A review of the literature (1980–2008)'. *SAHARA-J: Journal of Social Aspects of HIV & AIDS*, 6(1). 2–8.

National AIDSControl Organisation (NACO) (India). (1999). *National AIDS Control Programme Phase II (1999–2006)*, New Delhi: NACO.

National AIDSControl Organisation (NACO) (India). (2002). *National AIDS Prevention and Control Policy*. Retrieved from http://nacoonline.org/upload/Policies%20&%20Guidelines/NationalAIDSContyrol&PreventionPolicy2002.pdf.

National AIDSControl Organisation (NACO) (India). (2002a). *Handbook of Indicators for Monitoring National AIDS Control Programme II*. New Delhi: NACO and Ministry of Health and Family Welfare. Retrieved from http://library.cph.chula.ac.th/Ebooks.

National AIDSControl Organisation(NACO) (India). (2003). *National Blood Policy*, New Delhi: NACO and Ministry of Health and Family Welfare. Retrieved from http://upsacs.nic.in/bs%20doc/bs%20National%20Blood%20Policy.pdf.

National AIDSControl Organisation(NACO) (India). (2003a). *An Action Plan for Blood Safety*. New Delhi: NACO and Ministry of Health and Family Welfare.

National AIDSControl Organisation (NACO) (India). (2004). *National IEC/BCC Strategic Framework for HIV & AIDS Programme*. New Delhi: NACO and Ministry of Health and Family Welfare.

National AIDSControl Organisation(NACO) (India). (2004a). *Voluntary Counseling and Testing Operational Guidelines*. New Delhi: NACO and Ministry of Health and Family Welfare.

National AIDSControl Organisation(NACO) (India). (2004b). *National Guidelines for Implementation of Antiretroviral Therapy (ART) (Draft)*. New Delhi: NACO. Retrieved from http://nacoonline.org/upload/Policies%20&%20Guidelines/17,%20ART%20operational%20%20guidelines%202008.pdf.

National AIDSControl Organisation(NACO) (India). (2005). *Working Group Reports from NACP-III Consultations*. New Delhi: NACO.

National AIDS Control Organisation(NACO) (India). (2006). *National AIDS Control Programme Phase III (2006–2011): Strategic Implementation Plan*. New Delhi: NACO.

National AIDSControl Organisation(NACO) (India). (2007). *Operational Guidelines for Community Care Centres*. New Delhi: NACO.

National AIDS Control Organisation(NACO) (India). (2007a). *Ministry of Health & Family Welfare HIV Fact Sheets, Based on HIV Sentinel Surveillance Data in India*.

Retrieved    from    http://www.nacoonline.org/upload/NACO%20PDF/HIV_Fact_ Sheets_2006.pdf.

National AIDSControl Organisation(NACO) (India). (2009). *NACO Guidelines on Strengthening HIV & AIDS Interventions in the World of Work in India.* New Delhi: NACO. Retrieved from http://naco.gov.in/sites/default/files/15%2C%20NationalPoli cy-on-HIV-AIDS.pdf.

National AIDSControl Organisation(NACO) (India). (2010). *Red Ribbon Express: National AIDS Control Programme, Phase-III, India.* New Delhi: NACO and Ministry of Health and Family Welfare.

National AIDSControl Organisation(NACO) (India). (2011). *Condom Promotion. National AIDS Control Programme, Phase-III.* New Delhi: NACO and Ministry of Health and Family Welfare.

Naus, P., & Theis, J. (1991). 'The construction of sexuality: Implications for sex education and therapy'. *SIECCAN Journal,* 6. 19–24.

Nordenfelt, L. (1987). *On the Nature of Health.* London: Kluwer Academic Publishers.

Nuttavuthisit, K. (2007). 'Branding Thailand: Correcting the negative image of sex tourism', *Place Branding and Public Diplomacy,* 3(1). 21–30.

Ogden, J., Rangan, S., Uplekar, M., Porter, J., Brugha, R., Zwi, A., & Nyheim, D. (1999). 'Shifting the paradigm in tuberculosis control: Illustrations from India'. *The International Journal of Tuberculosis and Lung Disease,* 3(10). 855–861.

Osmond, M.W., & Thorne, B. (1993). 'Feminist theories: The social construction of gender in families and society'. In Boss, P.G., Doherty, W.J., LaRossa, R., Schumm, W.R., & Steinmetz, S.K. (Eds.). *Sourcebook of Family Theories and Methods: A Contextual Approach* (pp. 591–623). New York: Plenum.

Over, A.M. (2004). *HIV & AIDS Treatment and Prevention in India: Modeling the Costs and Consequences.* (Ed.). Washington, DC: World Bank Publications.

Panda, S. (2002). 'The HIV & AIDS epidemic in India: An overview'. In Panda, S. Chatterjee, A. & Abdul-Quader, A. (Eds.) *Living with the AIDS Virus: The Epidemic and the Response in India,* (pp. 17–35). New Delhi: SAGE.

Parker, R. (2000). 'Administering the epidemic: HIV & AIDS policy, models of development, and international health'. In Whiteford, L.M. & Manderson, L. (Eds.) *Global Health Policy, Local Realities: The Fallacy of the Level Playing Field.* (pp. 39–55). Boulder, CO: Lynn Renner Publishers.

Parker, R. (2002). 'The global HIV & AIDS pandemic, structural inequalities, and the politics of international health'. *American Journal of Public Health,* 92(3). 343–347.

Parker, R., & Aggleton, P. (2002). 'HIV & AIDS-related stigma and discrimination: A conceptual framework and an agenda for action'. *Population Council: Horizons Project.* Retrieved from www.popcouncil.org/pdfs/horizons/sdcncptlfrmwrk.pdf. Accessed on 01/09/2009.

Parkhurst, J.O. (2004). 'The political environment of HIV: Lessons from a comparison of Uganda and South Africa', *Social Science & Medicine,* 59(9). 1913–1924.

Pavarala, V. (1996). *Interpreting Corruption: Elite Perspectives in India.* New Delhi: SAGE Publications.

Penman, R. (2000). *Reconstructing Communicating: Looking to a Future.* Mahwah, NJ: Lawrence Erlbaum Associates.

Peterson, A. (1996). 'Risk and the regulated self: The discourse of health promotion as politics of uncertainty'. *Australian & New Zealand Journal of Sociology,* 32 (1). 44–57.

Pettegrew, L., & Logan, R. (1987). 'The health care context'. In Berger, C. & Chaffee, S. (Eds.). *Handbook of Communication Science*. Newbury Park, CA: SAGE.

Petty, R.E., & Cacioppo, J.T. (1986). *Communication and Persuasion: Central and Peripheral Routes to Attitude Change*. New York: Springer-Verlag.

Piotrow, P.T., Rimon, J.G., Payne Merritt, A., & Saffittz, G. (2003). *Advancing Health Communication: The PCS Experience in the Field*. Baltimore, MD: Johns Hopkins Bloomberg School of Public Health, Centre for Communication Programs. Retrieved from http://ccp.jhu.edu/documents/Advancing%20Health%20Communication-The%20PCS%20Experience%20in%20the%20Field.pdf.

Pitts, R.E., Whalen, D.J., O'Keefe, R., & Murray, V. (1989). 'Black and white response to culturally targeted television commercials: A value-based approach'. *Psychology and Marketing*, 6. 311–328.

Poku, N.K. (2001). 'Africa's AIDS crisis in context: "How the poor are dying"'. *Third World Quarterly*, 22. 191–204.

Polgar, M. (1996). 'Social constructions of HIV & AIDS: Theory and policy implications'. *Annual Review of Health Social Sciences*, 6. 81–111.

Press Information Bureau (PIB). (2010). Retrieved from www.pib.nic.in/newsite/erel content.aspx?relid=64510 accessed on 13/08/2018.

Prochaska, J.O., & Velicer, W.F. (1997). 'The Transtheoretical Model of health behavior change'. *American Journal of Health Promotion*, 12. 38–48.

Puri, J. (2002). 'Concerning Kamasutras: Challenging narratives of history and sexuality'. *Signs*, 27. 603–639.

Putzel, J. (2004). 'The global fight against AIDS: How adequate are the national commissions?' *Journal of International Development*, 16(8). 1129–1140.

Rao, T.S., & Avasthi, A. (2008). 'Roadmap for sexual medicine: Agenda for Indian Psychiatric Society'. *Indian Journal of Psychiatry*, 50(3). 153.

Richardson, D. (1998). 'Sexuality and citizenship. *Sociology*, 32(1). 83–100.

Richardson, D. (2000). 'Constructing sexual citizenship: Theorizing sexual rights'. *Critical Social Policy*, 20(1). 105–135.

Rimpela, M. (1998). 'Interplay of health care in Finland: An overview'. Paper presented at the XII World Congress of Pediatric and Adolescent Gynecology, Helsinki, Finland.

Robson, R., & Kessler, T. (2009). 'Unsettling sexual citizenship'. *McGill Law Journal*, 53, 2008.

Rogers, E., & Storey, J.D. (1987). 'Communication campaigns'. In Berger, C. & Chaffee, S. (Eds.). *Handbook of Communication Science*. Newbury Park, CA: SAGE.

Rogers, E.M. (1976). *Communication and Development: Critical Perspectives*. Hills, CA: SAGE.

Rogers, E.M. (2003). *Diffusion of Innovations* (3rd ed.). New York: Free Press.

Rokeach, M. (1969). *Beliefs, Attitudes, and Values: A Theory of Organization and Change*. San Francisco, CA: Jossey-Bass.

Romer, D., Black, M., Ricardo, I., Feigelman, S., Kaljee, L., Galbraith, J., Nesbit, R., Hornik, R.C., & Stanton, B. (1994). 'Social influences on the sexual behaviour of youth at risk for HIV exposure'. *American Journal of Public Health*, 84(6). 977–985.

Ross, M.W., & Carson, J.A. (1988). 'Effectiveness of distribution of information on AIDS: A national study of six media in Australia'. *The Journal of Urology*, 140(3). 697.

Sacks, V. (1996). 'Women and AIDS: An analysis of media misrepresentations'. *Social Science and Medicine*, 42(1). 59–73.

Salmon, C.T. (1986). 'Perspectives on involvement in consumer and communication research'. In Dervin, B. & Voigt, M. (Eds.). *Progress in the Communication Sciences* (pp. 243–268). Norwood, NJ: Ablex.

Sandfort, T.G., & Ehrhardt, A.A. (2004). 'Sexual health: A useful public health paradigm or a moral imperative?' *Archives of Sexual Behavior*, 33(3). 181–187.

Satcher, D. (2001). *The Surgeon General's Call to Action to Promote Sexual Health and Responsible Sexual Behavior*. Washington, DC: Office of the Surgeon General.

Schmidt, G. (1987). 'Sexual health within a societal context'. *Concepts of Sexual Health: Report of a Working Group*. ICP/MCH 521–523, 9614F.

Schramm, W. (1963). 'Communication development and the development process'. In Pye, L.W. (Ed.). (pp 30–57). *Communications and Political Development*. Princeton, NJ: Princeton University Press.

Seidman, S. (2001). 'From identity to queer politics: Shifts in normative heterosexuality and the meaning of citizenship'. *Citizenship Studies*, 5(3). 321–328.

Sethi, G. (2002). 'AIDS in India: The government's response'. In Panda, S.Chatterjee, A. & Abdul-Quader, A. (Eds.) *Living with the AIDS Virus: The Epidemic and the Response in India*, (pp. 36–61). New Delhi: SAGE.

Sibthorpe, B. (1992). 'The Social construction of sexual relationships as a determinant of HIV risk perception and condom use among injection drug users'. *Medical Anthropology Quarterly*, 6(3). 255–270.

Singhal, A., & Rogers, E.M. (1999). *Entertainment-Education: A Communication Strategy for Social Change*. Mahwah, NJ: Lawrence Erlbaum Associates Inc.

Singhal, A., & Rogers, E.M. (2001). 'The entertainment-education strategy in communication campaigns'. In Rice, R.E. & Atkin., C.K. (Eds.). *Public Communication Campaigns* (pp. 343–356). Thousand Oaks, CA: SAGE.

Singhal, A., & Rogers, E.M. (2002). 'A theoretical agenda for entertainment-education'. *Communication Theory*, 12(2). 117–135.

Singhal, A., & Rogers, E.M. (2003). *Combating AIDS: Communication Strategies in Action*. Thousand Oaks, CA: SAGE Publications.

Slovic, P. (1987). 'Perception of risk'. *Science*, 236. 280–285.

Solomon, S., Kumarasamy, N., Ganesh, A.K., & Amalraj, R.E. (1998). 'Prevalence and risk factors of HIV-1 and HIV-2 infection in urban and rural areas in Tamil Nadu, India'. *International Journal of STD & AIDS*, 9. 98–103.

Solon, O., & Barrazo, A.O. (1993). 'Overseas contract workers and economic consequences of the HIV and AIDS in the Philippines'. In Bloom, D.E. & Lyons, J.V. (Eds.). *Economic Implications of AIDS in South East Asia*. New Delhi: UNDP.

Sontag, S. (1991). *Illness as Metaphor/AIDS and its Metaphors*. London: Penguin Books.

Sood, S., Shefner-Rogers, C.L., & Sengupta, M. (2006). 'The impact of a mass media campaign on HIV/AIDS knowledge and behavior change in North India: Results from a longitudinal study'. *Asian Journal of Communication*, 16(3). 231–250.

Spector, M., & Kitsuse, J.I. (1977). *Constructing Social Problems*. Hawthorne, NY: Aldine de Gruyter.

Stake, R.E. (1995). *The Art of Case Study Research*. London: SAGE.

Sthapitanonda, P., Kunphai, K., Jatiket, P., & Jatiket, P. (2003). *Health Communication: The Potential of Mass Media for Health Promotion* (Thai language). Bangkok: Chulalongkorn University Book Centre.

Stillwagon, E. (2000). 'HIV transmission in Latin America: Comparison with Africa and policy implications'. *South African Journal of Economics*, 68(5). 985–1011.

Strain, L.A., & Chappell, N.L. (1982). 'Problems and strategies: Ethical concerns in survey research with the elderly'. *The Gerontologist*, 22. 526–531.

Strauss, A., & Corbin, J. (1990). *Basics of Qualitative Research: Grounded Theory Procedures and Techniques*. London: SAGE.

Stychin, C.F. (1998). *A Nation by Rights: National Cultures, Sexual Identity Politics, and the Discourse of Rights*. Philadelphia: Temple University Press.

Swaminathan, S., & Narendran, G. (2008). 'HIV and tuberculosis in India'. *Journal of Biosciences*, 33(4). 527–537.

Taylor, S.J., & Bogdan, R. (1984). *Introduction to Qualitative Research Methods: The Search for Meanings*. New York: John Wiley & Sons.

Temu, M.M., Changalucha, J.M., Mosha, F.F., Mwanga, J.R., Siza, J.E., & Balira, R. (2008). 'Community knowledge, attitude and practice towards sexually transmitted diseases and HIV infection in Biharamulo and Muleba districts in Kagera Region, Tanzania'. *Tanzania Journal of Health Research*, 10(4), 213–219.

Thompson, L. (1992). 'Feminist methodology for family studies'. *Journal of Marriage and the Family*, 54. 3–18.

Tiefer, L. (1987). 'Social constructionism and the study of human sexuality'. In Shaver, P. & Hendrick., C. (Eds.). *Sex and Gender*. Newbury Park, CA: SAGE.

Tiefer, L. (1995). *Sex Is Not a Natural Act and Other Essays*. Boulder, CO: Westview Press.

Tulloch, J. (1992). 'Using TV in HIV & AIDS education: Production and audience cultures'. *Media Information Australia*, 65(1). 10.

Tumushabe, J. (2006). *The Politics of HIV & AIDS in Uganda*. Programme Paper Number 28, United Nations Research Institute for Social Development, Social Policy and Development.

United Nations Development Programme (UNDP). (2004). *Thailand's Response to HIV & AIDS: Progress and Challenges* (pp. 22–24). Bangkok: UNDP.

United Nations General Assembly Special Session (UNGASS). (2012). *Country Report: Finland*. Helsinki: UNGASS.

United Nations General Assembly Special Session (UNGASS). (2012a). *Country Report: Lesotho*. Maseru: UNGASS.

United Nations General Assembly Special Session (UNGASS). (2012b). *Country Report: Netherlands and Parts of the Dutch Kingdom in the Caribbean*. Amsterdam: UNGASS.

United Nations General Assembly Special Session (UNGASS). (2012c). *Country Report: Swaziland*. Mbabane: UNGASS.

United Nations General Assembly Special Session (UNGASS). (2012d). *Country Report: Thailand*. Bangkok: UNGASS.

United Nations General Assembly Special Session (UNGASS). (2012e). *Country Report: Uganda*. Kampala: UNGASS.

United Nations Office on Drugs and Crime (UNODC). (2006). *Response for Prevention of HIV Among Drug Users in South Asia Through Opioid Substitution Treatment (OST)*. Vienna: UNODC.

United Nations Population Fund. (1994). 'Report of the International Conference on Population and Development, Cairo'. A/CONF. 171/13/Rev.1. Retrieved from www.unhcr.org/refworld/docid/4a54bc080.html.

United States Agency for International Development (USAID). (2004). *U.S. Foreign Aid: Meeting the Challenges of the Twenty-First Century*. Washington, DC: USAID.

Valente, T.W., & Saba, W.P. (1998). 'Mass media and interpersonal influence in a reproductive health communication campaign in Bolivia'. *Communication Research*, 25(1). 96–124.

Valente, T.W., Paredes, P., & Poppe, P.R. (1998). 'Matching the message to the process the relative ordering of knowledge, attitudes, and practices in behavior change research'. *Human Communication Research*, 24(3). 366–385.

Vance, C.S. (1991). 'Anthropology rediscovers sexuality: A theoretical comment'. *Social Science & Medicine*, 33(8). 875–884.

Velimirovic, B. (1987). 'AIDS as a social phenomenon'. *Social Science and Medicine*, 25(6). 541–552.

Vemula, R.K., & Gavaravarapu, S.M. (2017). *Health Communication in the Changing Media Landscape: Perspectives from Developing Countries*. (Eds). New York: Springer.

Villanueva, M.I.M. (1997). *The Social Construction of Sexuality: Personal Meanings, Perceptions of Sexual Experience, and Females' Sexuality in Puerto Rico*. Dissertation. Retrieved from http://scholar.lib.vt.edu/theses/available/etd13514459731541/unrestricted/DISSER1.PDF.

Visaria, L. (2000). 'From contraceptive targets to informed choice: The Indian experience', In Ramasubban, R. & Jejeebhoy, S.J. (Eds.) *Women's Reproductive Health in India*. (pp. 331–382). New Delhi: Rawat Publications.

Visaria, L., Jejeebhoy, S., & Merrick, T. (1999). 'From family planning to reproductive health: Challenges facing India'. *International Family Planning Perspectives*, 25. S44–S49.

Visaria, P., & Chari, V. (1998). 'India's population policy and family planning programme: Yesterday, today and tomorrow'. In Jain, A. (Ed.). (pp. 53–112). *Do Population Policies Matter? Fertility and Politics in Egypt, India, Kenya and Mexico*. New York: Population Council.

Viswanath, K., & Finnegan, J.R. (1995). 'The knowledge gap hypothesis: Twenty-five years later'. In Burleson, B. (Ed.). *Communication Yearbook 19* (pp. 187–228). Thousand Oaks, CA: SAGE.

Viswanath, K., & Finnegan, J.R. (2002). 'Reflections on community health campaigns: Secular trends and the capacity to effect change'. In Hornik, R. (Ed.). *Public Health Communication* (pp. 289–313). Mahwah, NJ: Lawrence Erlbaum Associates, Inc.

Weeks, J. (1998). 'The homosexual role after 30 years: An appreciation of the work of Mary McIntosh'. *Sexualities*, 1(2). 131–152.

Weinstein, N.D. (1993). 'Testing four competing theories of health-protective behavior'. *Health Psychology*, 12(4). 324.

Wilkins, K. (2000). *Redeveloping Communication for Social Change: Theory, Practice and Power*. Boulder, CO: Rowman and Littlefield.

Williams, K., & Miller, D. (1995). 'AIDS news and news cultures'. In: Downing, J., Mohammadi, A., & Sreberny-Mohammadi, A. (Eds.). *Questioning the Media - A Critical Introduction*. London: SAGE Publications.

Wilson, B.D., & Miller, R.L. (2003). 'Examining strategies for culturally grounded HIV prevention: A review'. *AIDS Education and Prevention*, 15(2). 184–202.

Wimmer, R., & Dominick, J. (1987). *Mass Media Research*. Belmont, CA: Wadsworth Publishing Company.

Wolffers, I. (1997). 'Culture, media, and HIV & AIDS in Asia'. *The Lancet*, 349. 52–54.

Wonders, N.A., & Michalowski, R. (2001). 'Bodies, borders, and sex tourism in a globalized world: A tale of two cities—Amsterdam and Havana'. *Social Problems*, 48(4). 545–571.

World Alzheimer Report. (2012). *Overcoming the Stigma of Dementia*. London: Alzheimer's Disease International (ADI).

World Bank. (2003). *Project Performance Assessment Report: India: National AIDS Control Project (Credit No 2350). Report No 26224*. Retrieved from http://lnweb90. worldbank.org/oed/oeddoclib.nsf/DocUNIDViewForJavaSearch/CF5907844F56853 D85256D900073CB1D/$file/India_PPAR_26224.pdf.

World Conference on Women: Action for Equality, Development and Peace on 4–15 September. (China). (1995). *Beijing Declaration*. Retrieved from www.un.org/wom enwatch/daw/beijing/platform/declar.htm.

World Health Organization (WHO). (1946). *Preamble to the Constitution of the World Health Organization*. World Health Organization. Retrieved from http://policy.who. int/.

World Health Organization (WHO). (1975). *Education and Treatment in Human Sexuality: The Training of Health Professionals. Technical Report Series No. 572*, Geneva: WHO.

World Health Organization (WHO). (1987). *Concepts of Sexual Health: Report of a Working Group*. Retrieved from http://whqlibdoc.who.int/euro/1993/ EUR_MUR_ 521.pdf.

World Health Organization (WHO). (1988). *Global Eradication of Poliomyelitis by the Year 2000*. Geneva: World Health Organization.

World Health Organization (WHO). (1994). *AIDS: Images of the Epidemic*. Geneva: World Health Organization.

World Health Organization (WHO). (2006). *Defining Sexual Health: Report of a Technical Consultation on Sexual Health 28–31 January 2002, Geneva*. Geneva: World Health Organization. Retrieved from www.who.int/reproductivehealth/p ublications/sexual_health/defining_sh/en/index.html.

World Health Organization (WHO)/Pan American Health Organization. (2001). *Promotion of Sexual Health: Recommendations for Action*. Proceedings of a Regional Consultation. Convened by Pan American Health Organization, World Health Organization in collaboration with the World Association for Sexology, Antigua, Guatemala.

Yep, G.A. (1993). 'HIV prevention among Asian–American college students: Does the Health Belief Model work?' *College Health*, 41(5). 199–205.

Yin, R.K. (2003). *Case Study Research: Design and Methods* (3rd Ed.). London: SAGE.

Yoshihara, S. (2009). 'Fatal misconception: The struggle to control world population, Mathew Connelly'. *National Catholic Bioethics Quarterly*, 8(4). 3–5.

Zhang, J. (2011). *The Rhetorics of Constructing HIV & AIDS in the United States and China: A Comparative Analysis of Two Online Discussion Forums*. Philadelphia, PA: Annenberg School of Communication, University of Pennsylvania.

# Index